The Up-To-Date Sandwich Book

THE UP-TO-DATE SANDWICH BOOK

400 Ways
to Make a Sandwich

By
EVA GREENE FULLER

CHICAGO
A. C. McCLURG & CO.
1909

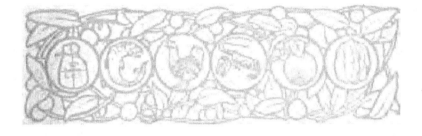

The Caslon Press
Chicago

CONTENTS

FOREWORD

THE first requisite in the preparation of good sandwiches is to have perfect bread in suitable condition. Either white, brown, rye, or entire wheat bread may be used, but it should be of close, even texture and at least one day old.

Cream the butter with a wooden spoon and spread smoothly on the bread before it is cut; after cutting remove the crust and avoid spreading the butter or filling over the edge. When ready to serve, cut the sandwiches either square, triangular, long, narrow, round, or crescent shaped.

In making rolled bread sandwiches, cut off the crust of a loaf of fresh bread and spread a thin layer of butter on one end of the loaf; cut off this buttered end in as thin a slice as possible and spread with the sandwich filling; roll up this slice and lay on a napkin; draw the napkin firmly around the rolled bread and pin it. Put in a cool place until ready to serve, then remove napkin and tie the sandwiches with baby ribbon or fasten with a tooth pick.

French rolls may be used for picnics and out-of-door luncheons. Remove from the top of each roll a piece of the crust the size of a silver dollar, and with a spoon take out the centre. Fill the space with highly seasoned chopped meat, fish, lobster, or crab, replace lid, wrap in tissue paper, and serve with pickles or olives.

For very small, dainty sandwiches to be served at afternoon teas or luncheons, the bread may be baked at home in pound baking powder cans. These should be only half filled, and then allowed to rise before baking. You then have a round slice without crust.

A garnish such as the following may be used: For meat sandwiches, use pickles, olives, lettuce, watercress, parsley, and mint. For fish sandwiches, use pickles, olives, cress, parsley, slices of lemon, and hard-boiled egg. For cheese sandwiches, use pickles and olives. For sweet sandwiches, use lettuce, maiden hair fern, smilax, berries, flowers, and candied fruit.

To keep sandwiches fresh, if prepared an hour or two before serving, wring out a napkin in cold water and cover the tray and keep in a cool place or wrap in wax paper.

FISH

THE UP-TO-DATE SANDWICH BOOK

FISH

OYSTER SANDWICH

Chop raw oysters fine, add a dash of tabasco sauce, lemon juice, and oil. Season with pepper and salt. Spread this on thinly cut slices of white bread, with a lettuce leaf between.

FRIED OYSTER SANDWICH

On thin slices of lightly buttered white bread, place a lettuce leaf that has been dipped in mayonnaise dressing. Place fried oysters on lettuce leaf. Put slices together and garnish with a pickle.

DEVILED OYSTER SANDWICH

Cut slices of bread thin, remove crust, and toast. Cover a slice with oysters, dust thickly with red pepper and spread lightly with mayonnaise. Cover with another slice of toast. Garnish with a slice of lemon.

OYSTER LOAF SANDWICH

Cut Vienna rolls into halves and spread lightly with butter; on one half lay four fried oysters, cover with the other half of roll, and serve with a pickle.

OYSTER AND CAVIARE SANDWICH

Butter thin slices of brown bread, cover one slice thinly with caviare and on this lay two raw whole oysters; cover with another slice of bread and garnish with slice of lemon.

GRILL ROOM OYSTER SANDWICH

Toast three slices of white bread and lightly butter. Place fried oysters between the slices and dust lightly with pepper and salt. Cut in strips and serve on a lettuce leaf. Remove contents of half an orange peel and fill with chili sauce. Serve on the plate with the sandwich.

OYSTER SALAD SANDWICH

Chop fine two stalks of celery and one medium sized cucumber; add one cup of cold cooked oysters cut in pieces, mix with one-half cup of cream dressing. Place on thin slices of lightly buttered white bread with a crisp lettuce leaf between.

CAVIARE SANDWICH

Between thin slices of buttered rye bread, spread caviare; on top of that sprinkle a little finely chopped onion. Garnish top with a slice of lemon.

CAVIARE SANDWICH NO. 2

To a can of caviare add the juice of half a lemon, and one teaspoonful of olive oil. Mix well together until a paste is formed. Spread mixture on thin slices of lightly buttered white bread or toast and cover with another slice of bread.

CAVIARE—LOBSTER SANDWICH

Spread thinly buttered white bread with caviare, season with lemon juice, and on top of this lay a little minced lobster. Cover with another slice of buttered bread and place on a lettuce leaf.

ROE SANDWICH

Mix the yolks of three hard-boiled eggs with the roe of a salt herring. Place the mixture between thin slices of lightly buttered white bread. Garnish with a slice of lemon.

SHAD-ROE SANDWICH

One set of shad-roe that has been cooked and pounded in a mortar, the yolks of five hard-boiled eggs chopped very fine, two teaspoonfuls of finely chopped capers, a dash of paprika, and two tablespoonfuls of tabasco sauce. Mix and place between thin slices of lightly buttered white bread.

SHAD-ROE AND CUCUMBER SANDWICH

Marinate one cup each of cucumber and cooked shad-roe, and a dash of mayonnaise and place on a crisp lettuce leaf between thin slices of lightly buttered white bread.

LOBSTER SANDWICH

On thin slices of lightly buttered white bread lay a crisp lettuce leaf; on top of that place shredded meat of a boiled lobster that has been mixed with a little mayonnaise dressing. Cover with another slice of bread and press together.

LOBSTER SANDWICH NO. 2

Cut the meat of a cold boiled lobster into dice. Sprinkle with a little salt, red pepper, and a tablespoonful of tarragon vinegar. Add three tablespoon-

fuls of melted butter. Place mixture on slices of lightly buttered whole wheat or brown bread, cover with another slice of bread, press the two together, remove the crusts, and cut into triangles. Garnish with an olive.

LOBSTER SANDWICH NO. 3

Pound the meat of a medium sized lobster fine, add one tablespoonful of the coral, dried and mashed smooth, the juice of half a lemon, a dash of nutmeg, one-fourth teaspoonful of paprika, and two tablespoonfuls of soft butter. Mix all to a smooth paste and place between thin slices of lightly buttered white bread.

LOBSTER SANDWICH NO. 4

Chop the meat of a medium sized lobster and a stalk of celery fine, moisten with a little mayonnaise dressing, and place between thin slices of lightly buttered white bread. Garnish with a slice of lemon.

LOBSTER SALAD SANDWICH

Mix one cup of lobster meat with a little mayonnaise dressing. Marinate crisp lettuce leaves and arrange on thin slices of lightly buttered white bread; cover with lobster, and cover lobster with bread; sprinkle lobster coral on top. Prepare just before serving.

DUTCH LUNCH SANDWICH

Take two square salted crackers and place on one two thin slices of Bermuda onion, next a layer of sardines and squeeze a generous amount of lemon juice over all; then put remaining cracker (buttered) on top. Salmon may be substituted.

LOBSTER AND MUSHROOM SANDWICH

Cook one-half pound of mushrooms in a little butter until tender, then add one small sliced onion,

moisten with a little stock and let simmer until done. Remove from the fire and chop fine; press through a sieve and season with salt and pepper and a dash of tomato catsup. When cool, add a little lobster meat pounded smooth, mix and spread on thin slices of lightly buttered white bread. Garnish with an olive.

SARDINE SANDWICH

Remove the skin and bones from two boxes of sardines, and pound the meat to a paste. Add a teaspoonful of anchovy paste, a dash of salt and red pepper, and rub in the yolks of six hard-boiled eggs, with two tablespoonfuls of olive oil. Spread mixture on toasted bread. To be eaten while toast is hot.

SARDINE SANDWICH NO. 2

Remove scales and bones from two boxes of sardines. Put the sardines in a mortar with the yolks of five hard-boiled eggs. Pound fine; add one table-

spoonful of olive oil, the juice of one-half lemon, a
pinch of mustard, a dash of pepper and salt, two sprigs
of finely chopped watercress. When smoothly blended
spread the mixture between thin slices of lightly buttered white or graham bread.

SARDINE SANDWICH NO. 3

Remove scales and bones from two boxes of sardines. Four hard-boiled eggs, chopped fine, the juice
of one lemon, a dash of salt, red and black pepper, a
tablespoonful of melted butter, a sprig of parsley,
chopped fine. Stir to a paste and spread on lightly
buttered white bread with a lettuce leaf between.

SARDINE SANDWICH NO. 4

Remove skin and bones from the sardines and
pound to a paste; season with salt and cayenne pepper
and a dash of lemon juice. Spread on thin slices of
lightly buttered white or rye bread; cover with another slice of bread and garnish with a pickle.

SARDINE SANDWICH NO. 5

Pound eight boned and skinned sardines with two ounces of fresh butter, a little salt and cayenne. Spread the mixture on slices of brown bread lightly buttered, and over them lay a slice of skinned tomato. Sprinkle with salt and pepper and a pinch of sugar. Add a few drops of lemon juice. Form into sandwiches and cut into finger lengths.

SARDINE AND CHEESE SANDWICH

Equal parts of boned and skinned sardines and cream cheese mashed to a pulp. Mix and place between thin slices of white or rye bread. Garnish with a pickle.

SARDINE CLUB SANDWICH

Three slices of thinly cut white bread, toasted and buttered. Place a lettuce leaf that has been dipped in mayonnaise dressing on the lower slice, and on top

of that put slices of broiled breakfast bacon, then put
another slice of toast on top of that, with another lettuce leaf followed by boneless and skinless sardines
split open, topped by a third slice of toasted bread.
Garnish with slices of lemon cut very thin and dipped
in finely chopped parsley.

SPANISH SANDWICH

. Cut slices of white bread rather thick and toast;
trim off crusts and lightly butter. Remove skin and
bone from the sardines and lay them on the toast.
Sprinkle chopped olives over the sardines and the
juice of a quarter of a lemon. Cover with another
slice of buttered toast. Serve on a lettuce leaf.

BROILED SARDINE SANDWICH

Use sardines in oil, remove from can and put on
a platter to drain off oil. Toast thin slices of bread
and cut in triangles or squares, and butter while hot.
Dip each sardine in cracker crumbs, put on a broiler

19

and broil over a coal fire first on one side, then the other. Lay two broiled sardines on a piece of toast, cover with another slice, and garnish with a slice of lemon. Serve as soon as made.

AUSTRIAN SANDWICH

Two cans of boned and skinned sardines, two balls of cottage cheese, one small onion chopped fine, two tablespoonfuls of chopped parsley, two tablespoonfuls of chopped mint, two tablespoonfuls of vinegar, salt to taste, a dash of red pepper, the grated rind and juice of two lemons; also use the oil from the sardines. Mix and beat thoroughly; spread between thin slices of lightly buttered rye or brown bread.

SALMON SANDWICH

Between thin slices of lightly buttered white bread, place a crisp lettuce leaf; on that put canned salmon that has been seasoned with salt and pepper and a dash of lemon juice. Garnish with a slice of lemon.

SALMON SANDWICH NO. 2

One can of salmon, two sticks of celery chopped fine, juice of half a lemon, a dash of salt, and a teaspoonful of melted butter. Mix and place between thin slices of lightly buttered white bread, cut in fancy shapes. Garnish with a sprig of parsley.

SALMON SANDWICH NO. 3

One can of salmon, one small head of lettuce chopped fine. One teaspoonful of melted butter, a dash of salt, and juice of half a lemon. Mix and place between thin slices of buttered white bread. Garnish with an olive.

SALMON SANDWICH NO. 4

Flake the salmon and moisten with mayonnaise dressing. Use as a filling between thin slices of brown bread lightly buttered. Garnish with a slice of lemon that has been dipped in finely chopped parsley.

SALMON AND HAM SANDWICH

One-half can of salmon, two slices of cold boiled ham, two sprigs of watercress. Chop these together until fine, add a dash of lemon juice. Place between thinly cut slices of buttered bread.

PIMENTO SANDWICH

Grind two small cans of pimentos with two cakes of Neufchatel cheese, and season with a little salt. If the mixture is too dry add a little oil of pimentos. Spread on thin slices of lightly buttered white bread. Place two together and cut in fancy shapes.

SHRIMP SANDWICH

Minced cold shrimp, a celery stick chopped fine; add a little mayonnaise dressing, a dash of salt. Mix and spread on thin slices of rye bread lightly buttered. Press slices together and garnish with an olive.

SHRIMP SALAD SANDWICH

Marinate one cup of shrimps with French dressing; add one-half cup each of chopped olives and pimentos; drain, moisten with mayonnaise dressing, and place on thin slices of lightly buttered white bread, with a crisp lettuce leaf between.

LENTEN SANDWICH

Whip a cup of cream until stiff, stir in minced cold shrimp, a little parsley, a dash of salt and pepper. Spread mixture between thin slices of white or graham bread. Garnish with an olive.

CRAB SANDWICH

Take the contents of a small can of crab meat, squeeze out liquor; mix with a little mayonnaise dressing. Place a crisp lettuce leaf on each slice of lightly buttered white bread, and spread with crab mixture. Put slices together and cut in squares.

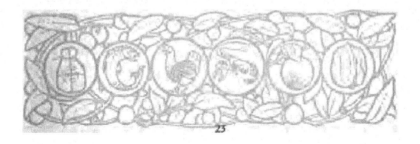

MOCK CRAB SANDWICH

One-fourth cupful of grated American cheese, two tablespoonfuls butter creamed, a dash of salt, paprika, and mustard, a teaspoonful of chopped olives, vinegar and anchovy paste. Mix and spread on thin slices of white bread. Put the two slices together.

ANCHOVY SANDWICH

Pour off wine, then wash thoroughly in vinegar. Allow them to soak in olive oil for a half-hour, remove, open lengthwise, and take out bones; place between thin slices of unbuttered bread. Garnish with an olive.

ANCHOVY SANDWICH NO. 2

A can of boneless anchovies mixed with three hard-boiled eggs, chopped fine. Add a dash of lemon juice, a teaspoonful of melted butter, a pinch of salt. Mix and spread on lightly buttered white bread, with a lettuce leaf between. Garnish with a pickle.

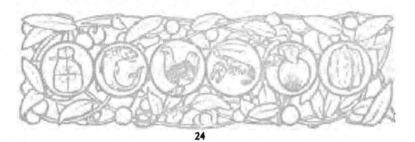

FISH SANDWICH

To cold cooked fish, minced fine, add a little chopped pickle. Season with pepper and salt. Place between two slices of buttered white bread.

FISH AND EGG SANDWICH

Mix with an equal amount of cold cooked fish the yolks of hard-boiled eggs, mixed to a paste; add a little mayonnaise dressing. Spread mixture on lightly buttered white bread with a lettuce leaf between.

SARDELLEN PASTE SANDWICH

Wash, bone, and skin one-half pound of sardellen and mash to a paste. Rub together the yolks of two hard-boiled eggs and one teaspoonful of butter until smooth, then add the sardellen paste. Mix and spread on small squares of buttered toast. Serve with an olive.

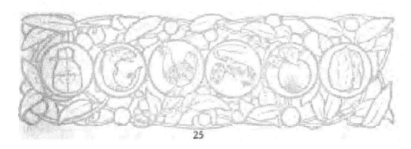

SARDELLEN SANDWICH

Clean, bone, and mash smooth, one-half pound sardellen, mix with one tablespoonful of creamed butter, and juice of half a lemon, a dash of white pepper, and a half-teaspoonful of prepared mustard. Spread on thin slices of round toast, cover with another slice, and garnish with a pickle.

HALIBUT SANDWICH

Cold halibut shredded, mixed with a little mayonnaise dressing and capers. Spread between lightly buttered white bread. Garnish with a radish.

HALIBUT SANDWICH NO. 2

Shred boneless cold boiled halibut and rub smooth with a wooden spoon; season with salt and pepper and one tablespoonful of lemon juice; add three tablespoonfuls of thick cream and toss up. Spread

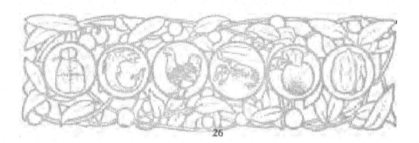

this mixture on thin slices of lightly buttered white bread, with a crisp lettuce leaf, that has been dipped in mayonnaise dressing, between. Cut triangular.

ANCHOVY TOAST

One can of boneless anchovies in oil; toast squares pf bread without crusts to a nice even brown; two anchovies are placed between two slices of toast and the yolks of hard-boiled eggs are chopped fine and sprinkled over same, the whites being cut into cubes and disposed over the top; dust with white pepper. Garnish with a slice of lemon.

FRENCH SANDWICH

To one pint of cold cooked fish, add two hard-boiled eggs chopped fine, two tablespoonfuls of capers,

and a little mayonnaise to moisten. Mix and spread on thin slices of lightly buttered white bread, cover with another slice, and cut in strips. Add a sprinkling of finely chopped cress to the top of each sandwich; rub the yolk of a hard-boiled egg through a sieve and chop the white very fine. Add a sprinkling of the yolk to the cress on half the number of sandwiches, adding the white to the other half. Then arrange them in groups of twos, one of each color on the serving plate. Any cold meat may be used instead of the fish.

HOT CREAMED CODFISH
SANDWICH

Between toasted and lightly buttered slices of white bread place hot creamed codfish. Put a table-spoonful of the codfish on top and sprinkle finely chopped hard-boiled egg over the codfish and garnish with a sprig of parsley and a pickle. Serve as soon as made.

E G G

EGG SANDWICH

Chop finely the whites of hard-boiled eggs; force the yolks through a potato ricer; mix yolks and whites, season with salt and pepper, and moisten with a little mayonnaise dressing. Place mixture between thin slices of lightly buttered white bread with a lettuce leaf between. Garnish with an olive.

EGG SANDWICH NO. 2

Slice cold hard-boiled eggs and lay them between very thin, buttered slices of white bread, seasoning them with salt, pepper, and nutmeg. Garnish with a pickle.

FRIED EGG SANDWICH

Fry eggs well done, add a dash of salt and pepper, and place between thin slices of white bread, with a crisp lettuce leaf between. Garnish with a radish.

RIBBON SANDWICH

Mash the yolks of five hard-boiled eggs to a paste, add three tablespoonfuls of mayonnaise dressing and pepper and salt to taste. Spread lightly with butter three square thin slices of white bread and two corresponding slices of wheat. For lower slice use the white bread and spread with the egg paste, then place the wheat bread on top of that and spread with the egg paste, followed by a slice of the white bread. Press tightly together, then take a sharp knife and cut crosswise into five sandwiches. Garnish with an olive.

EGG AND LETTUCE SANDWICH

Place slices of hard-boiled eggs to cover slices of thinly cut buttered white bread, add a dash of salt and paprika, on this lay a crisp leaf of lettuce that has been dipped in mayonnaise dressing; cover with the other buttered slice of bread and cut diagonally in halves. Garnish with an olive.

EGG AND OLIVE SANDWICH

Chop five hard-boiled eggs very fine. Stone and chop fifteen large olives and mix with the egg, moisten all with three tablespoonfuls of melted butter, season with salt and pepper, and mix to a moist paste. Spread on thin slices of lightly buttered white bread. Put two slices together and garnish with an olive.

EGG AND CUCUMBER SANDWICH

Run a sour cucumber pickle through the meat chopper, then run through six hard-boiled eggs. Mix with a little mayonnaise dressing. Place mixture between thin slices of lightly buttered white bread with a crisp lettuce leaf between.

EGG AND BROWN BREAD SANDWICH

Chop hard-boiled eggs fine, season with salt and pepper, add olive oil until of the consistency to spread. Use for a filling for brown bread sandwiches.

PURITAN SANDWICH

Rub smooth the yolk of a hard-boiled egg, add a tablespoonful of melted butter, a dash of salt and white pepper, one-half teaspoonful of mustard and one-fourth of a pound of American cheese grated, then stir in a scant tablespoonful of vinegar. Spread mixture on thin slices of lightly buttered white or rye bread. Put two slices together and garnish with a pickle.

GOLD SANDWICH

Rub the yolks of three hard-boiled eggs to a paste. Add two tablespoonfuls of olive oil, mixing with a silver fork. Add a pinch of mustard, cayenne pepper and salt, and lastly one tablespoonful of vinegar. When this is thoroughly mixed, add one cup of grated American cheese. Spread on thin slices of lightly buttered white bread.

MONTPELIER SANDWICH

Put three hard-boiled eggs and three boned anchovies in a mortar and pound fine; add one ounce of butter, and season with salt and cayenne pepper. Place between thin slices of white bread cut in fancy shapes. Garnish with a sprig of parsley.

JAPANESE EGG SANDWICH

Chop four hard-boiled eggs and three boned sardines fine, add a teaspoonful of melted butter and rub to a paste; season with pepper and salt and a little mayonnaise dressing; cut in slender strips. Garnish with parsley and an olive.

BROWN EGG SANDWICH

Mash the yolks of five hard-boiled eggs and moisten with a teaspoonful of melted butter and a drop of vinegar, work to a paste, adding salt, pepper and a little French mustard, and a drop of tabasco. Spread

the mixture between slices of lightly buttered Boston brown bread cut wafer thin. Garnish with an olive.

EASTER SANDWICH

Between thin slices of lightly buttered white bread, place a crisp lettuce leaf that has been dipped in mayonnaise dressing. On this place round slices of cold hard-boiled egg. Dust with pepper and salt. Cut sandwiches in squares and tie with lavender baby ribbon.

CHEVY CHASE SANDWICH

Put six hard-boiled eggs through a potato ricer. To these add six sweet pickles, chopped fine, a dash of salt and white pepper, and two teaspoonfuls of melted butter; mix and place between thin slices of lightly buttered white bread.

OUTING SANDWICH

Chop hard-boiled eggs fine, season with salt and pepper; moisten with mayonnaise dressing. Spread on buttered whole wheat bread. Garnish with a pickle.

TRAVELLER'S SANDWICH

Chop hard-boiled eggs fine, add a few minced olives, season with lemon juice; mix with butter, creamed. Spread on thin slices of white bread.

CURRIED EGG AND OYSTER SANDWICHES

Chop four boiled eggs very fine, season with pepper and salt and spread on thin slices of lightly buttered white bread; on top of eggs place three pickled oysters; over this spread a tablespoonful of curry sauce and cover with another slice of bread. The sauce is made thus; put a tablespoonful of butter into a sauce pan, add a cup of milk, thicken with a little flour dissolved in a little cold milk, let come to a boil, then add a dash of onion juice, salt and pepper, and a teaspoonful of curry. Let simmer a minute, then set it aside to cool. When sandwiches are ready to serve, spread this sauce over the egg and oysters, then cover with the other slice of bread. Garnish with parsley.

SALADS

TOMATO SANDWICH

Pare, chill, and cut ripe tomatoes thin, season with salt and pepper and a little lemon juice. Place between thin slices of lightly buttered white bread with a crisp lettuce leaf between.

TOMATO SANDWICH NO. 2

On thin slices of lightly buttered white bread place a crisp lettuce leaf that has been dipped in mayonnaise dressing; on this, place thin slices of tomato, add a dash of salt, and spread lightly with mayonnaise dressing; cover with another lightly buttered slice of bread.

TOMATO AND ONION SANDWICH

Mix in a bowl some tomato catsup, season with pepper and salt and a pinch of sugar, add a little finely chopped onion, mix and place between thin slices of buttered white. bread, with a crisp lettuce leaf between.

TOMATO AND HORSE-RADISH SANDWICH

Slice a tomato thin and sprinkle with salt. Mix one-half cup of horse-radish with two tablespoonfuls of mayonnaise dressing. Spread thin slices of lightly buttered white bread with the horse-radish mixture, and put the sliced tomato between.

TOMATO AND NUT SANDWICH

Chop three medium sized tomatoes, add one small green pepper chopped fine, and a half-cup of chopped walnuts; add a dash of mayonnaise dressing and place on a lettuce leaf between thin slices of white bread cut in squares.

SPECIALTY SANDWICH

On thin slices of toasted bread that have been lightly buttered, place a thick slice of tomato, over top of tomato spread salad dressing, then just a touch of caviare, cover with another slice of toast, and garnish with a slice of lemon.

EPICUREAN SANDWICH

Two medium sized tomatoes, three green sweet peppers, and one small onion, chop fine, mix together, salt, and drain in sieve for five minutes. Mix with a little salad dressing and place on a lettuce leaf, between thin slices of white or whole wheat bread lightly buttered.

BEET SANDWICH

Chop cold boiled beets fine, season with salt and pepper and a dash of vinegar. On thin slices of lightly buttered white bread, spread cream cheese. On top of this sprinkle the chopped beets. Cover with another slice of bread.

BEET AND CHEESE SANDWICH

Slice bread thin. Spread one piece with beets that have been chopped very fine and moistened with mayonnaise dressing. The other spread with cream cheese. Press slices firmly together.

WATERCRESS SANDWICH

Dip fresh leaves of watercress in mayonnaise dressing. Place between thin slices of white bread lightly buttered.

WATERCRESS AND EGG SAND-WICH

Chop cress and moisten with French dressing. Press the yolks of three hard-boiled eggs through a colander and add to the mixture. Place between thin slices of lightly buttered white bread.

WATERCRESS AND EGG SAND-WICH NO. 2

Cut watercress into small pieces, removing the stalks, and mix with finely chopped hard-boiled eggs, seasoned with salt and pepper. Place between thin, buttered slices of bread, sprinkling the cress and egg very lightly with lemon juice. Press together, and cut in squares, removing the crusts.

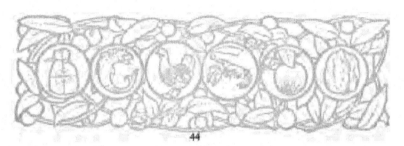

MUSHROOM SANDWICH

Boiled mushrooms chopped fine, cold boiled tongue chopped fine, season with pepper and salt, add a little mayonnaise dressing, mix, and spread between thin slices of buttered white bread. Garnish with an olive.

WESTERN SANDWICH

Chop five olives, a dozen capers, and one gherkin fine and mix with two tablespoonfuls of mayonnaise dressing. Spread the lower slices of buttered white bread with fresh cream cheese, season with salt and pepper, then put another slice on top of that and spread with the olive mixture. On top place a third slice, press together, cut round, and garnish with a sprig of parsley.

PICCALILLI SANDWICH

Between thinly cut slices of lightly buttered white bread, place a layer of sweet piccalilli; cut in diamond shape. Garnish with a sprig of parsley.

GREEN PEPPER AND EGG SANDWICH

Between thinly cut slices of lightly buttered white bread, place seedless green peppers that have been chopped fine and mixed with a little mayonnaise dressing. On top of that place slices of hard-boiled egg. Garnish with a sprig of parsley and a small pickle.

NASTURTIUM SANDWICH

Spread thin slices of lightly buttered white bread with mayonnaise dressing; place nasturtium blossoms overlapping one another half way; roll up the sandwich and fasten with a toothpick.

RIPE OLIVE SANDWICH

Chop ripe olives fine, mix with a little mayonnaise, and place between thin slices of lightly buttered white bread.

OLIVE SQUARES

Cut thin squares of brown bread and lightly butter, adding a dash of pepper and salt. Stone eight olives, chop them with two stalks of celery, one tiny cucumber pickle, a teaspoonful of catsup, a dash of salt and pepper, and a very little mustard. Mix well and spread on the brown bread, covering with another square.

OLIVE AND PEPPER SANDWICH

Chop olives fine, add a little finely chopped green and red (sweet) peppers, a dash of mayonnaise dressing; mix and place between thin slices of lightly buttered white bread.

OLIVE AND CHICKEN LIVER SANDWICH

Chop olives and cold boiled chicken livers fine; mix with mayonnaise and spread on thin slices of whole wheat bread. Put the slices together.

OLIVE AND CHEESE SANDWICH

Thin slices of white bread lightly buttered, cut in hexagon shape. Between each two slices place a layer of Neufchatel cheese mixed to a paste with a little thick cream and mayonnaise dressing, and cover thickly with chopped olives.

OLIVE AND CAPER SANDWICH

Stone the olives and chop fine, adding one-third quantity of capers, mix with a little mayonnaise dressing, and spread between thin slices of lightly buttered white bread.

OLIVE AND CAPER SANDWICH NO. 2

Chop equal amount of capers and olives fine, season with celery salt and paprika, add a little olive oil or melted butter, mix until smooth. Spread on slices of lightly buttered white bread.

OLIVE AND NUT SANDWICH

Chop olives and English walnuts fine, add a dash of mayonnaise dressing, and spread on lightly buttered brown bread.

CUCUMBER SANDWICH

Peel cucumbers and cut into the thinnest possible slices and sprinkle with salt and pepper and a few drops of lemon juice. Place between thin slices of lightly buttered bread.

CUCUMBER SANDWICH NO. 2

Sprinkle thin slices of lightly buttered white bread with cayenne. Place thinly sliced cucumbers that have been mixed with a little French dressing between the slices.

CUCUMBER SANDWICH NO. 3

Soak thin slices of cucumber for one hour in good white vinegar, season with salt and pepper. Place between thin slices of buttered brown bread. Cut in strips.

CUCUMBER SANDWICH NO. 4

Chop cucumbers fine, add a pinch of salt and pepper and a dash of French dressing. Mix and place between thin slices of lightly buttered white bread, with a crisp lettuce leaf between.

CUCUMBER AND CHIVES SAND-WICH

On thin slices of lightly buttered white bread, place thin slices of cucumber, over which sprinkle chopped chives; cover with another slice of bread and cut in squares.

CUCUMBER AND CHEESE SAND-WICH

Slice cucumbers thin, let stand in salt water ten minutes, drain, and place slices on thinly buttered white bread. Sprinkle with grated American cheese, put slices together, and garnish with a radish.

CUCUMBER AND RED PEPPER SANDWICH

Chop three medium sized cucumbers and one red pepper, add a little mayonnaise dressing, and place between thin slices of lightly buttered white bread.

CUCUMBER AND ONION SAND-WICH

Chop fine one large cucumber and a small white onion. Add a dash of pepper and salt and moisten with a little mayonnaise dressing. Place between thin slices of lightly buttered Boston brown bread.

DILL SANDWICH

Lightly butter slices of white bread; cover half of them with thin slices of the white meat of roasted chicken; put over this a thin layer of dill pickles; cover with another slice of buttered bread, trim off the crusts, cut in triangles, and serve on a lettuce leaf.

SPINACH SANDWICH

Chop cold boiled spinach and the yolks of hard-boiled eggs fine, add a dash of salt and vinegar. Spread between thin slices of buttered white bread. Garnish with a pickle.

ONION SANDWICH

Slice a mild sweet onion and lay in salted ice water for a half-hour. Mix with a good mayonnaise dressing, and place slices of onion between well buttered slices of Boston brown bread cut thin.

MUSTARD SANDWICH

Cream two tablespoonfuls of butter with one tablespoonful of prepared mustard. Spread a thin layer between thinly cut slices of rye bread. Garnish with a pickle.

MOSAIC SANDWICH

White, brown, and graham bread are used for this sandwich. Cut the slices thin and spread with green butter. The butter is made by putting cold boiled spinach through a sieve, season with finely chopped parsley and capers, and mix smooth with creamed butter. Put slices together.

HORSE-RADISH SANDWICH

Cream two tablespoonfuls of butter, add three tablespoonfuls of prepared horse-radish, spread between exceedingly thin slices of white bread. Garnish with parsley; serve as soon as made.

CELERY SANDWICH

Chop fine a few stalks of celery, mix with a little mayonnaise dressing, spread on thin slices of lightly buttered bread, cover with another slice.

CELERY SANDWICH NO. 2

Butter bread on the loaf, first having creamed the butter. Cut away the crusts and starting at one corner of the slice, roll it over two crisp short celery sticks. Tie with baby ribbon.

CELERY AND ENGLISH WALNUT SANDWICH

Mix one cup of chopped celery, one-fourth cup of chopped English walnuts, and one-fourth cup chopped olives. Moisten with mayonnaise and place between thin slices of lightly buttered brown bread.

CELERY AND ENGLISH WALNUT SANDWICH NO. 2

Chop celery and English walnuts fine, add a dash of salt and allspice, moisten with a little mayonnaise dressing. Spread between thin slices of lightly buttered white bread.

LETTUCE SANDWICH

Between thin, oblong slices of lightly buttered white bread, place a crisp lettuce leaf that has been dipped in mayonnaise dressing, and sprinkled with Parmesan cheese.

LETTUCE SANDWICH NO. 2

Cut crisp lettuce leaves into ribbons with scissors, add a dash of mayonnaise dressing, and season with salt. Place between thin slices of lightly buttered white or brown bread.

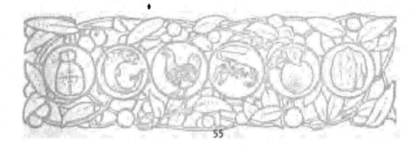

BOSTON BROWN BREAD SAND-WICH

Between thin slices of lightly buttered brown bread place a lettuce leaf that has been dipped in mayonnaise dressing.

BAR HARBOR SANDWICH

Cut the crisp lettuce leaves into ribbons with the scissors, salt and pepper and moisten with a little mayonnaise dressing. Place on thin slices of lightly buttered white bread; on each lay a thin slice of tomato and cover with another slice of buttered bread. Press together and serve as soon as made.

RADISH SANDWICH

Between thin slices of lightly buttered white bread place sprigs of watercress and thin slices of a radish that has been dipped in French dressing. Can be served with the fish course.

STRING BEAN SANDWICH

Cook string beans until tender; when cold, cut in small pieces, add a chopped onion, and a few chopped English walnut meats. Mix with a little French dressing and spread between lightly buttered slices of white bread, with a crisp lettuce leaf between.

APPLE AND CELERY SANDWICH

Chop three apples and three stalks of celery fine. Mix with a little mayonnaise dressing and place on thin slices of lightly buttered white bread. Put the two slices together.

APPLE AND GRAPE SANDWICH

Remove the seeds from thin skinned white grapes; add one apple and one stalk of celery; chop fine. Moisten with French dressing, toss up, and spread on thinly cut slices of buttered white bread. Place the two slices together.

APPLE SALAD SANDWICH

Chop fine two medium sized red apples and two stalks of celery; mix with a little boiled dressing and place between thin slices of buttered white bread.

WALDORF SANDWICH

Chop two apples, two stalks of celery, and one sweet pepper fine, add a little mayonnaise dressing, mix, and place between thin slices of lightly buttered white bread. Garnish with a sprig of watercress.

NOVELTY SANDWICH

Chop one small onion, eight olives, one green pepper (seeds removed), and one chow chow pickle fine. Add one cupful of grated Parmesan cheese; moisten with enough mustard dressing from the chow chow to form a paste. Spread on thin slices of lightly buttered white bread. Cover with another slice and cut in triangles.

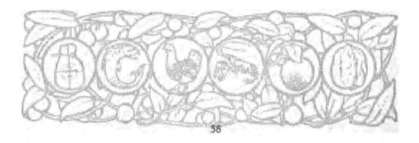

ST. PATRICK SANDWICH

Chop a handful of mint, a handful of parsley, and a tiny onion very fine, add a dash of paprika, mix with a little mayonnaise dressing. Place between thin slices of lightly buttered white bread. Garnish with a sprig of parsley.

TARTAR SANDWICH

Take two tablespoonfuls each of chopped onion, parsley, capers, and sour cucumber pickles. Mix with two tablespoonfuls of mayonnaise dressing. Place mixture between thin slices of graham or white bread lightly buttered.

GRAPE FRUIT SANDWICH

Remove the pulp from grape fruit, making one cup; add one-fourth cup of finely chopped walnuts, moisten with a little mayonnaise dressing, and place between thin slices of lightly buttered white bread cut in strips.

CHERRY SALAD SANDWICH

Remove stones from two cups of cherries, add one-half cup of English walnuts and two stalks of celery that have been chopped fine; add enough mayonnaise to moisten; place between thin slices of lightly buttered white bread. Garnish with a cherry.

PINEAPPLE SALAD SANDWICH

Shred one medium sized pineapple, add one cupful of skinned and seeded white grapes, one-half cup of finely chopped English walnuts; moisten with cream mayonnaise. Place between thin slices of lightly buttered white bread with a crisp lettuce leaf between. Garnish with a red cherry.

MOCK OYSTER SANDWICH

Boil salsify until tender, work smooth with a little sweet cream, season with salt, cayenne, and a dash of anchovy sauce; place between thin slices of lightly buttered white bread.

MEAT

ROAST BEEF SANDWICH

Two cups of cold boiled beef chopped fine; add a tablespoonful of tomato catsup, a dash of pepper and celery salt, two tablespoonfuls of melted butter, and a teaspoonful of vinegar. Mix well and spread on lightly buttered white bread. Put the two slices together and garnish with an olive.

ROAST BEEF SANDWICH NO. 2

Between thin slices of buttered bread place thin slices of cold roast beef; spread this thinly with horse-radish.

HOT ROAST BEEF SANDWICH

Between thin slices of lightly buttered white bread place a thin slice of hot roast beef. Put two tablespoonfuls of brown gravy over top. Garnish with a pickle.

ROAST BEEF AND TOMATO SAND-WICH

Lightly butter thin slices of Boston brown bread, cover with a thin layer of cold roast beef, lightly spread with mayonnaise dressing; put on top of this a slice of tomato, dust with pepper and salt, cover with another slice of bread. Serve on lettuce leaves.

ROAST BEEF AND JAM SAND-WICH

Between thin slices of lightly buttered white bread, place thin slices of cold roast beef; on top of this spread plum jam.

ROAST BEEF SALAD SANDWICH

Chop fine one cup of cold roast beef, one-half head of lettuce, one boiled beet, one hard-boiled egg, one small onion, and one pickled cucumber. Mix with French dressing and place between thin slices of lightly buttered white bread.

RARE BEEF SANDWICH

To two parts of chopped lean rare beef, add one part of finely minced celery. Season with salt, pepper, and a little made mustard. Place on a lettuce leaf between thin slices of lightiy buttered white bread.

CORNED BEEF SANDWICH

Chop cold corn beef very fine, season with mustard and a dash of catsup. Place mixture on a lettuce leaf, between lightly buttered white bread.

CHIPPED BEEF SANDWICH

Chop chipped beef very fine and mix with a little mayonnaise; spread on thin slices of lightly buttered white bread.

PICNIC SANDWICH

A pound of raw beef run through the meat chopper; a teacupful of bread crumbs, pepper and salt to taste; mix with a well-beaten egg, and form into a roll.

Take a flank of mutton, remove the bones and lay the above mixture on the mutton and do it up into a roll; bind it with a tape. Sew up the ends so mixture will not bulge out; dust with pepper and salt, then roast it; when it is cold, take off the tape, take out the sewing, and slice thin. Place between thin slices of lightly buttered white bread. Garnish with an olive.

CANNIBAL SANDWICH

Chop raw beef and onions very fine, season with salt and pepper, and spread on lightly buttered brown bread.

MEAT AND MUSHROOM SAND-WICH

Mince boiled mushrooms and cold beef or tongue together, and spread between thin slices of lightly buttered white bread. Lightly spread the filling with French mustard. Garnish with a pickle.

FRIED COLD MEAT SANDWICH

Place between thin slices of white bread, cold roast beef or lamb, chopped fine; season with pepper and salt. Mix with a little of the left-over gravy; dip in egg and milk and fry brown in butter. Serve hot.

BROILED STEAK SANDWICH

Between slices of lightly buttered white bread, place a thin piece of hot broiled steak, season with salt and pepper. Garnish top with a thin slice of Bermuda onion.

HAM SANDWICH

Grind boiled ham fine; mix with a little chopped celery and mayonnaise. Place between slices of thinly cut buttered bread.

HAM SANDWICH NO. 2

Chop ham fine, mix with a little mayonnaise dressing, and place between thin slices of lightly buttered white bread. Garnish with parsley and a pickle.

HAM SANDWICH NO. 3

Slice cold boiled ham thin; spread with French mustard, place between thin slices of rye bread. Garnish with a pickle.

HAM SANDWICH NO. 4

One pound of cold boiled ham run through fine knife or meat chopper, one-half cup strained lemon juice, mix with a little mayonnaise dressing, spread on thin slices of lightly buttered white bread, with a crisp lettuce leaf between.

HOT HAM SANDWICH

Spread thin slices of white bread with chopped cold boiled ham, over same spread a little mustard, and cover with another slice. Beat an egg and add one-half cup of milk, and in this mixture dip the sandwiches. Garnish with parsley and a pickle.

HOT HAM SANDWICH NO. 2

Spread finely minced boiled ham on thin slices of lightly buttered bread. Put the sandwiches together and cut into triangles. Beat two eggs light, add a cup of milk and a pinch of salt. Dip the sandwiches in the egg and milk and fry brown on a hot buttered griddle. Garnish with a slice of broiled tomato and serve at once.

HAM FINGERS

Run lean ham through the meat chopper, season with salt and pepper, and moisten with a little salad dressing. Place the ham between slices of thinly cut and lightly buttered bread. Cut in shape of lady fingers and garnish with a sprig of watercress.

HAM AND EGG SANDWICH

Chop cold boiled ham and hard-boiled eggs fine, season with pepper and salt, and a dash of mayonnaise dressing. Place the mixture between thin slices

of lightly buttered brown bread. Garnish with a small pickle.

HAM AND EGG CLUB SANDWICH

Chop cold boiled ham very fine and rub smooth in a mortar; pass the yolks of four hard-boiled eggs through a sieve and add a little mayonnaise dressing. Cut white bread very thin and lightly butter; on one slice spread the ham, then cover with another slice, and on that spread the egg mixture with a crisp lettuce leaf between, topped by a third slice of lightly buttered bread. Garnish with a pickle.

HAM AND NUT SANDWICH

Mince finely some cold boiled ham and add to it about half the quantity of finely chopped peanuts. For every cupful of ham add a tablespoonful of chopped pickles and a little chopped celery. Mix to a paste with salad dressing and spread on thin slices of lightly buttered white bread and serve on a lettuce leaf.

70

POTTED HAM SANDWICH

Between thin slices of lightly buttered white
bread spread potted ham; remove crusts and shape
them in triangular form. Garnish top with a radish.

POTTED HAM SANDWICH NO. 2

Toast saltine biscuit, lightly butter, and spread
with potted ham. Put two together, serve as soon as
made. Garnish with a pickle.

PARTY SANDWICH ROLLS

Fresh bread is used for these sandwiches. Cut
the slices as thin as possible and remove the crusts. Lay
crisp lettuce leaves that have been dipped in mayonnaise
dressing on the slices; on top of that place thin shav-
ings of cold boiled ham; roll the slices very closely and
fasten with a toothpick or ribbon. Pile on a serving
dish and garnish with pickles and radishes.

WESTPHALIAN HAM SANDWICH

Between thin slices of lightly buttered rye bread, place thin slices of Westphalian ham; add a dash of mustard, and garnish top with a pickle.

AUTOMOBILE SANDWICH

Run through the meat chopper two pounds of cold boiled ham, half a pound of walnut meats, and four dill pickles. Mix with a little French mustard, and place between slices of lightly buttered bread.

STAG SANDWICH

Run cold boiled ham and dill pickle through the meat chopper, add a little French mustard, and spread on thin slices of lightly buttered white bread. Cover with another slice.

BOSTON CLUB SANDWICH

Cut brown bread into rounds with a cake cutter and lightly butter. Chop one-half pound of cold boiled mutton fine; add a dash of salt and pepper, two table-spoonfuls of olive oil, or melted butter. On the lower round of buttered bread place a small crisp lettuce heart that has been dipped in mayonnaise dressing. On top of that place a slice of tomato, then another slice of buttered bread, then the mutton mixture. Place on top another round of buttered bread and press the two together.

VEAL SANDWICH

Grind through meat chopper the desired amount. To one cup of chopped meat add one tablespoonful of vinegar, one-half teaspoonful of mustard, one-half of a small onion chopped fine. Salt and pepper to taste. Mix to a paste with mayonnaise dressing, and place between thin slices of lightly buttered white bread. Garnish with a pickle.

CALF'S LIVER SANDWICH

Chop cooked calf's liver fine, add crisp fried bacon chopped fine. Season with salt and pepper, add a dash of catsup; mix and place on lettuce leaves between thin slices of buttered white bread.

CALF'S LIVER AND BACON SAND-WICH

Calf's liver well cooked and chopped fine, slices of bacon fried crisp and chopped fine; season with salt and pepper and a dash of catsup. Mix and place on thin slices of lightly buttered graham or white bread, with a crisp lettuce leaf between.

TEXAS SANDWICH

Chop one-half pound of broiled calf's liver fine. Season with salt and cayenne pepper, add on teaspoonful of melted butter and a few drops of onion juice; rub together to a smooth paste. Spread on thin slices of unbuttered white bread. Cover with another slice.

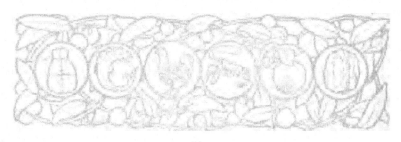

TONGUE SANDWICH

Between thin slices of lightly buttered white bread, lay a crisp lettuce leaf that has been dipped in mayonnaise dressing; on that lay a thin slice of tongue; on top of that a slice of ripe tomato spread with mayonnaise.

TONGUE SANDWICH NO. 2

Mince boiled tongue, add a teaspoonful of melted butter, a tablespoonful of tomato catsup, a dash of celery salt, and when mixed place between thinly buttered white or brown bread. Serve with a sweet pickle.

TONGUE AND EGG SANDWICH

Chop cold boiled tongue fine; season with salt and pepper and a tablespoonful of melted butter; mix and spread on rounds of toasted bread. Place leaves of watercress around edge on top of the toast and in the centre pile hard-boiled egg that has been chopped fine and mixed with a little mayonnaise dressing.

DEVILED TONGUE SANDWICH

Run a quarter of a pound of cold boiled tongue through the meat chopper; add to it three hard-boiled eggs chopped fine, a dash of red pepper and paprika, a teaspoonful of Worcestershire sauce, and two table-spoonfuls of melted butter. Mix and place between thin slices of lightly buttered bread with sprigs of watercress between.

TONGUE AND TOMATO SAND-
WICH

Lightly butter three thin slices of white bread. On lower slice place a lettuce leaf that has been dipped in mayonnaise dressing; on leaf place a slice of cold boiled tongue, then a slice of bread; on this lay a slice of tomato that has been dipped in mayonnaise dressing, topped by a third slice of bread. Garnish with an olive.

EXCURSION SANDWICH

Chop cold boiled tongue fine. To each cupful, add two tablespoonfuls of melted butter, a dash of red pepper, and one-half teaspoonful of onion juice. Mix and spread on very thin slices of white bread, cover with another slice, and serve with a pickle.

LAMB SANDWICH

To three cups of cold cooked lamb, chopped fine, add three tablespoonfuls of Parmesan cheese, one teaspoonful of mustard, a dash of salt and pepper, and a little mayonnaise dressing; mix until smooth. Place this on lettuce leaf between slices of lightly buttered white bread.

LAMB SANDWICH NO. 2

Chop cold cooked lamb and a green pepper fine. Season with salt and add a dash of mayonnaise dressing. Spread on thin slices of graham bread lightly buttered. Put the two slices together.

MUTTON SANDWICH

Chop cold boiled mutton fine, add a dash of tabasco sauce, a teaspoonful of olive oil or melted butter, a tablespoonful of vinegar, and a pinch of salt. Spread on lightly buttered white bread. Serve with a pickle.

MUTTON SANDWICH NO. 2

Chop cold cooked mutton very fine; to each pint add one teaspoonful of salt, one tablespoonful of capers, on teaspoonful of chopped mint, a dash of pepper, and one tablespoonful of lemon juice. Spread this thickly over whole wheat bread. Cover with another slice and serve on lettuce leaves.

MUTTON AND PEA SANDWICH

Butter slices of white bread lightly and lay on them thin slices of cold boiled mutton. Mix together half a pint of cooked peas that have been seasoned with salt, pepper, a little butter, and a teaspoonful of capers. Place a layer of peas over the mutton, then a crisp lettuce leaf, then cover with another slice of buttered bread, and cut into triangles.

SUMMER SANDWICH

Cut white bread into rounds with a cake cutter and lightly butter. Chop one-half pound of cold boiled mutton fine; add two tablespoonfuls of melted butter, and a dash of salt and pepper. Peel four tomatoes, cut these into rather thick slices and remove the seeds from the centre. Place a lettuce leaf that has been lightly dipped in mayonnaise dressing on a slice of toast, and put a slice of tomato on top of that. Fill the space from which you have taken the seeds with the mutton mixture. Put on top another slice of toasted and lightly buttered bread, and press the two slices firmly together.

POTTED MEAT SANDWICH

Chop one pound of tender cooked veal fine and add one-fourth cup of fat pork cooked and chopped fine. Season with salt and pepper, a little anchovy essence, and a little mace. Moisten with a little butter and work until smooth. Press the mixture solidly into small can or jar, pour melted butter to the depth of one-half inch over same, and set in a cool place. When ready for use, slice and place between thin slices of white bread. Garnish with a pickle.

FARMER SANDWICH

Between thin slices of white bread, place thin slices of cold roast pork; on top of this spread apple sauce.

PORK SANDWICH

Chop cold boiled pork and a celery stalk fine; season with salt, add a dash of Worcestershire, slightly diluted with water; mix and place between thin slices of buttered white bread.

MINCE-MEAT SANDWICH

Moisten thick round crackers with hot milk; spread with a thick layer of hot mince meat, made rather moist with the addition of a little fruit juice or syrup. Place another cracker on top, then whipped cream on top of that. To be eaten with a fork.

SOUTHERN (BACON) SANDWICH

On thin slices of buttered whole wheat bread, place a lettuce leaf; add thin slices of crisp fried bacon; spread with a little mustard, and put slices together. Garnish with a radish.

TIP-TOP SANDWICH

Chop fine six slices of uncooked bacon, add two green peppers (seeds removed) chopped fine, three onions the size of an egg chopped fine, season with pepper and salt. Fry the above mixture until the bacon is done, then scramble in two eggs. Place between thin slices of lightly buttered white bread. Garnish with a radish.

CHICKEN SANDWICH

Two cups of finely minced cold cooked chicken, a heaping tablespoonful of Parmesan cheese, a tablespoonful of tomato catsup, a dash of French mustard, salt and pepper, add a little thick cream, work all to a smooth paste. Place between thin slices of buttered white bread. Garnish with a stick of celery.

CHICKEN SANDWICH NO. 2

To the white meat of a cold boiled chicken chopped fine, add a crisp celery stalk chopped fine, and mix with a little mayonnaise dressing. Place between thinly cut slices of buttered white bread, and garnish with an olive.

CHICKEN SANDWICH NO. 3

Chop cold cooked chicken fine; season with pepper and salt, add a dash of mayonnaise dressing, spread on thinly cut slices of buttered white bread, with a lettuce leaf between, and garnish with an olive.

CHICKEN SANDWICH NO. 4

One cup of cold boiled chicken chopped fine; season with salt and paprika, moisten with a little cream, paste between thin slices of lightly buttered whole wheat bread.

HOT CHICKEN SANDWICH

Between thin slices of lightly buttered toast, place slices of warm chicken breast; over same pour hot gravy, made of slightly thickened chicken stock, seasoned with salt and pepper, and a little chopped parsley. Cut triangular and garnish with a pickle, and a radish.

CHICKEN LIVER SANDWICH

Boil chicken liver until tender and rub through a sieve; mix with an equal amount of olives chopped fine, and mayonnaise dressing; place between thin slices of lightly buttered white bread.

PRESSED CHICKEN SANDWICH

Boil fowl until tender; remove bones and skin; chop fine; season with salt, pepper, and sage to taste. Mix teaspoonful of mustard with a tablespoonful of vinegar, heat and pour over chicken, with some of the broth, and press in earthen dish. When cold and ready for use, slice and place between thin, lightly buttered bread with a crisp lettuce leaf between.

JELLIED CHICKEN SANDWICH

Chop the white meat of cold boiled chicken fine, rub to a paste. Put a scant tablespoonful of gelatine in a half-cup of cold water, place it over the fire until it has dissolved; then add the chicken paste, a dash of salt and pepper, and a half-teaspoonful of grated horseradish. Stir this mixture until it begins to thicken, then stir in one cup of cream that has been whipped to a stiff froth, place it in the ice box until very cold; when ready for use, cut thin and place between lightly buttered slices of crustless white bread. Garnish with parsley and an olive.

CREAM OF CHICKEN SANDWICH

Take one cupful of chopped chicken and pound it fine; dissolve a tablespoonful of gelatine in a half-cup of cold water; then add the chicken meat, a dash of salt, a teaspoonful of grated horse-radish; stir until it begins to thicken, then add a little at a time, one-half pint of cream that has been whipped to a stiff froth; set in the ice box until very cold. On thin slices of lightly buttered white bread, spread the mixture; cut in fancy shapes and garnish each with a radish.

CHICKEN AND EGG SANDWICH

One cupful of cold chicken chopped fine; the yolks of two hard-boiled eggs chopped fine; one teaspoonful of melted butter, one teaspoonful of lemon juice, one teaspoonful of rich stock, and salt and pepper to taste. Mix to a paste and spread on thin slices of lightly buttered white bread. Garnish with an olive.

CHICKEN SURPRISE SANDWICH

Chop cold boiled chicken and few capers fine; . mix with a little mayonnaise dressing and spread between thin slices of toasted white bread. Garnish with an olive.

CHICKEN AND HAM SANDWICH

One cupful of chopped ham, one cupful of cold boiled chicken meat; season with salt and pepper and moisten with mayonnaise dressing. Spread this mixture on thin slices of lightly buttered white bread, cover with another slice, and cut in halves. Garnish with a pickle.

CHICKEN AND HAM (CLUB) SAND-WICH

Toast and lightly butter three thin slices of white bread; place a lettuce leaf that has been dipped in mayonnaise dressing on the lower slice. On this, place

slices of cold roast fowl, then put another slice of toast on top of that, with another leaf of lettuce, follow by thin slices of broiled ham, topped by a third slice of toasted bread. Garnish top with dill pickle, cut in thin slices lengthwise.

CHICKEN AND ENGLISH WALNUT SANDWICH

Spread thin slices of buttered white bread with English walnut or almond meats chopped fine. Spread the corresponding pieces with cold boiled chicken chopped fine; add a little mayonnaise dressing and press pieces together. Garnish with an olive.

CHICKEN AND ALMOND SAND-WICH

One cup of cold boiled chicken chopped fine; one cup of almonds chopped fine; moisten with a little cream, season with salt and paprika, place between thin slices of entire wheat bread. Garnish with parsley, and an olive.

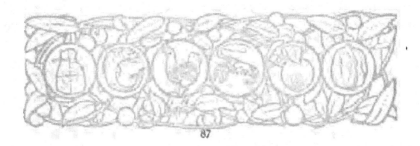

CHICKEN AND GREEN PEPPER SANDWICH

Run enough chicken through the meat chopper to make two cupfuls; cut out the stem ends and remove the seeds from three large sweet peppers; run them through the meat chopper; mix the chicken and pepper together; season with half a teaspoonful of salt, and two tablespoonfuls of sweet cream. Place between thin slices of lightly buttered white bread. Cut in triangles. Serve on lettuce leaf.

ASPIC JELLY SANDWICH

Soak one box (two ounces) of gelatine in one cup of chicken liquor until softened; add three cupfuls of chicken stock seasoned with a little parsley, celery, three cloves, a blade of mace, and dash of salt and pepper. Strain into a dish and add a little shredded breast of chicken; set in a cold place to harden; when cold, slice in fancy shapes and place on slightly buttered whole wheat bread. Garnish with a stick of celery.

RECEPTION SANDWICH

Equal quantities of breast of cold boiled chicken and tongue, put through food chopper; season with celery salt, cayenne, anchovy paste, and mayonnaise. Place mixture between slices of lightly buttered white bread with crisp lettuce leaf that has been dipped in tarragon vinegar.

QUEEN SANDWICH

Mince finely two parts of cooked chicken or game to one part of cooked tongue, and one part of minced cooked mushrooms. Season with salt and pepper and a little lemon juice; mix and place between thin slices of buttered white bread. Garnish with small pickle.

FRENCH ROLL SANDWICH

French rolls are used for this sandwich. Make a small round opening in top of each and take out some of the crumbs; save the small crusts from the top of

the opening; chop fine five olives, a tablespoonful of capers, one green sweet pepper (seeds removed), one gherkin, the white meat of one chicken, and two ounces of tongue chopped fine. Moisten with mayonnaise dressing. Fill this mixture into the roll, put the small crust on top, and garnish with a pickle.

CREOLE SANDWICH

One cupful of cold boiled chicken chopped fine, two tablespoonfuls of green pepper that has been parboiled and chopped fine. Add a dash of salt, and a teaspoonful of chopped parsley; moisten with a little mayonnaise dressing and place between thin slices of lightly buttered white bread. Garnish with an olive.

WINDSOR SANDWICH

One cupful of cold boiled chicken chopped fine, a teaspoonful of finely chopped onion, a half teaspoonful of finely chopped chives. Salt and pepper to taste,

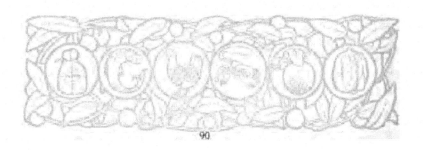

moisten with a little mayonnaise dressing, mix well, and spread on thin slices of toasted bread. Cover with another slice of toasted bread, cut in halves, and garnish with a radish.

BISCUIT SANDWICH

Roll biscuit dough very thin, about like piecrust, and spread with butter, then roll another and put on top of this; cut out and bake in quick oven. When done, pull apart and spread with this mixture while warm. Take equal parts of chicken and ham, run through the meat chopper, season with celery salt and cayenne pepper; moisten with mayonnaise dressing.

SARATOGA SANDWICH

On a lightly buttered square slice of white bread, place a lettuce leaf that has been dipped in mayonnaise dressing; on that lay four large fried oysters with a little horse-radish on top of the oysters, and cover

with a lightly buttered slice of rye bread, and butter upper side of this slice. On this lay a slice of breast of cooked chicken; dust with salt and pepper and lay on that crisp slices of fried bacon; cover this with a slice of white bread. Garnish top with radishes, cut fancy, serve with slice of lemon on the side.

SHERIDAN PARK CLUB SANDWICH

Toast and butter three thin slices of white bread; place a lettuce leaf on the lower slice, and on its top put slices of chicken breast. Then put another slice of toast on top of that with another leaf of lettuce, followed by thin slices of broiled breakfast bacon, topped by third slice of toasted bread. Garnish top with small pickles cut in slices lengthwise. Serve as soon as made.

COLONIAL (CLUB) SANDWICH

Toast and butter three slices of thinly cut bread; place slices of cold boiled chicken spread lightly with mayonnaise dressing on the lower slice, with a crisp lettuce leaf. Then put another slice of toast on top of

that with a slice of ripe tomato spread lightly with mayonnaise dressing, topped by a third slice of toast spread with finely chopped celery that has been mixed with a little mayonnaise dressing. Lay on top of that sweet red peppers cut in ribbons; cut triangular.

CHICKEN AND PÂTÉ DE FOIE GRAS SANDWICH

Two tablespoonfuls *pâté de foie gras* and a cup of finely chopped cold boiled chicken; season with pepper and salt; spread on a crisp lettuce leaf that has been dipped in French dressing, and place between thin slices of white bread.

CHICKEN BISCUIT FINGER

Chop cold boiled chicken very fine; add a little chopped parsley; moisten with salad dressing; make rolls of the mixture about the size of a small pickle. Cover each roll with baking powder biscuit dough rolled thin, pressing the ends tightly. Brush with beaten egg and bake.

PRESSED MOCK CHICKEN

Boil a piece of fresh shoulder of pork until tender, adding pepper and salt to the water in which it is cooked. When done, run the meat through the meat chopper and return to the liquor in which it was boiled in the kettle. Add enough rolled oats to absorb or thicken the liquid, season to suit the taste, and simmer from twenty to thirty minutes; then pack into a bowl or crock; when cold, slice and place between thin slices of lightly buttered white bread. Garnish with pickles and radish roses.

COUNTRY CLUB SANDWICH

Use three slices of white bread thinly cut and lightly buttered; place a lettuce leaf that has been dipped in mayonnaise dressing on lower slice, and on top of that place slices of cold boiled chicken; then put another slice of bread and a lettuce leaf followed by thin slices of veal loaf, topped by another slice of bread with thinly sliced pickles on top.

CHICAGO CLUB SANDWICH

Toast.lightly two slices of white bread and one of rye; lightly butter and on the slices of white bread, place slices of cold cooked chicken and a couple of slices of bacon well crisped; cover with the slice of rye bread and on that place a lettuce leaf that has been dipped in a little mayonnaise dressing; sprinkle with a little chopped green pepper, then cover with the other slice of white bread.

TURKEY SANDWICH

Between thin slices of lightly buttered white or brown bread, place thin slices of turkey breast; spread a little cranberry jelly over this and sprinkle with finely chopped celery.

HOT TURKEY SANDWICH

Between thin slices of lightly buttered toast, place slices of warm turkey breast; over same pour a hot gravy made of slightly thickened turkey stock. Garnish with a pickle.

TURKEY CLUB SANDWICH

Toast three thin slices of white bread and butter, on the lower slice lay cold white breast of turkey; cover with another slice of toast; on that lay a thin slice of hot broiled ham; cover with another slice of buttered toast and press together. Serve on a lettuce leaf. Garnish with small pickles.

GAME SANDWICH

On thin slices of lightly buttered bread, place slices of breast of roasted partridge; spread lightly with currant jelly and cover with another buttered slice of bread. Garnish with cress.

TRUFFLE SANDWICH

One tablespoonful of broiled truffle, one-half breast of chicken, and two tablespoonfuls of sweetbreads chopped fine. Add a dash of mayonnaise dressing, salt and pepper. Place between slices of buttered white bread, cut in oblong pieces. Garnish with pickle.

HEAD CHEESE SANDWICH

Between thin slices of lightly buttered white bread, place a lettuce leaf that has been dipped in mayonnaise dressing. On this place thin slices of head cheese, cut diagonally, and garnish with a pickle.

SWEETBREAD SANDWICH

Cook sweetbreads until tender. When cold, remove skin, chop fine, season with salt and pepper, add one cup of finely chopped celery, and a dash of mayonnaise dressing; spread on thin slices of lightly buttered white bread. Cover with another slice and garnish with an olive.

SAUSAGE SANDWICH

Boil link sausages until done; when cold cut into thin slices; place between thin slices of lightly buttered white bread. Garnish with a pickle.

GERMAN BOLOGNA SANDWICH

Remove the skin from a bologna sausage and rub to a paste. Spread thin slice of lightly buttered rye bread with a little French mustard, then a layer of bologna, cover with another slice, and garnish with a pickle.

FRANKFURT SAUSAGE SAND-WICH

Cut cold boiled Frankfurt sausage into the thinnest slices and place on slice of buttered white or rye bread; run a cucumber pickle through a meat chopper and sprinkle on top of sausage. Place another buttered slice over this.

SALAMI (ITALIAN SAUSAGE) SANDWICH

Between slices of lightly buttered rye bread, place thin slices of salami. Garnish with an olive.

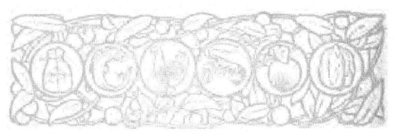

PÂTÉ DE FOIE GRAS is made from the liver of geese, ducks, or turkeys. Put one-half cup goose grease in a fryer on stove; when hot lay in the livers and baste with a spoon until tender; remove the livers from the pan and chop very fine. Add a small onion chopped and boiled brown, season with salt and pepper and mix in some of the grease in which livers were fried. The mixture must resemble paste. *Pate de foie gras* can be purchased in small cans.

PÂTÉ DE FOIE GRAS SANDWICH

On thin slices of toasted bread shorn of crusts, spread *pâté de foie gras;* add a dash of salt and cayenne; cover with another slice of toast and serve with a sweet pickle.

PÂTÉ DE FOIE GRAS SAND-
WICH NO. 2

Three slices of white or brown bread lightly buttered; on the lower slice spread *pâté de foie gras*, then put another slice of bread on top of that. Cover with delicate shreds of tomato, tiny lettuce hearts with a dash of mayonnaise dressing, topped by a third slice of bread. Garnish with an olive.

PÂTÉ DE FOIE GRAS SAND-
WICH NO. 3

One-half cup of *pâté de foie gras,* remove the fat and mash to a smooth paste; season with a little salt and a dash of cayenne pepper and drop of onion juice; press the whole through a sieve. Spread on thin slices of buttered white bread and cover with another slice of buttered bread. Garnish top with slices of hard-boiled egg and an olive.

IMITATION PÂTÉ DE FOIE GRAS
SANDWICH

Saute half a chopped onion in butter until brown; add one-half dozen chicken livers, cover with seasoned chicken stock, and let simmer until tender; mash the livers fine and press through a sieve, season with salt, paprika, mustard, and a dash of curry powder. Put this paste in a cup, pour melted butter over top; when cold, remove the butter and cut in thin slices; place between thin slices of white bread. Garnish with a pickle.

CHEESE

AMERICAN CHEESE SANDWICH

Cream three tablespoonfuls of butter, add three tablespoonfuls of grated American cheese, one tablespoonful of anchovy essence, a dash of salt and paprika, one-fourth teaspoonful of mustard, and one-fourth cupful of finely chopped olives. Place mixture between thin slices of lightly buttered rye bread.

AMERICAN CHEESE SANDWICH NO. 2.

Cream two tablespoonfuls of butter, add one-fourth cupful of grated American cheese and one teaspoonful of vinegar, and season with salt, paprika, mustard, and anchovy essence. Place mixture between thin slices of white bread. Garnish with a pickle.

AMERICAN CHEESE SANDWICH NO. 3

Salted cracker slightly toasted, spread with American cheese; serve hot.

AMERICAN CHEESE SANDWICH
NO. 4

Melt a quarter of a pound of American cheese in a sauce pan, add the yolk of one egg beaten with two tablespoonfuls of cream, a dash of salt and red pepper, and half a teaspoonful of Worcestershire sauce. Take from the fire and when cold, spread on thin slices of white or rye bread. Press the two together and cut in strips. Garnish with a pickle.

CHEESE RAREBIT SANDWICH

Grate a quarter of pound of American cheese fine; melt it in a sauce pan over the fire, add the yolks of two eggs well beaten, two tablespoonfuls of cream, a dash of salt and red pepper, and a teaspoonful of Worcestershire. Stir the mixture into the melted cheese; when blended, remove from the fire, and when cool, spread it on thin slices of lightly buttered white bread. Put the two slices together and garnish with an olive.

BROWN BREAD AND AMERICAN CHEESE SANDWICH

Steam the brown bread before spreading with butter, and cut in the usual way. Between the slices, place grated American cheese and finely chopped English walnuts well salted. Garnish with an olive.

BROWN BREAD AND AMERICAN CHEESE SANDWICH NO. 2

Cut thin small rounds of brown bread and lightly butter; sprinkle with grated cheese; put two slices together and cut in two.

FRIED CHEESE SANDWICH

Cut slices of white bread round with biscuit cutter; spread with paste made with half a cupful of fresh American cheese, mashed smooth with a little cream. Season with salt and paprika. Put slices together and fry a light brown in the blazer, in which a tablespoonful of butter has been melted. Serve hot.

NEUFCHATEL SANDWICH

Mince a little candied orange very fine, add a dash of ginger, and mix with Neufchatel cheese which has been moistened with a little cream. Place between thin slices of lightly buttered white bread. Garnish with an olive.

NEUFCHATEL AND NUT SAND-WICH

Mix with one roll of Neufchatel cheese, half a cupful of chopped almonds or butternuts; spread on thin slices of lightly buttered graham or Boston brown bread. Garnish with a small pickle.

NEUFCHATEL AND OLIVE SAND-WICH

Chop half a dozen olives and a half-cupful of pecan meats fine; mix with a cake of Neufchatel cheese, moisten with a little cream, and place between thin slices of lightly buttered white bread.

HARLEQUIN SANDWICH

Lightly buttered slices of white and graham bread. Spread each with Neufchatel cheese and sprinkle with a few English walnut meats. Put a white and a brown slice together.

BERLIN SANDWICH

Chop olives fine and moisten with mayonnaise dressing; spread on buttered slices of bread. Spread other slices with Neufchatel cheese and put slices together in pairs.

LIMBURGER CHEESE SANDWICH

Spread thin slices of lightly buttered rye bread with limburger cheese, then with thin slices of bologna sausage; cover with another slice of rye bread. Garnish with a pickle.

ROQUEFORT SANDWICH

Mix grated cheese with thick cream to make a paste; place between thinly cut slices of lightly buttered white bread. Garnish with an olive.

GERMAN CLUB SANDWICH

Thin slices of pumpernickel, rye, and white bread are used for this sandwich. Rub half a pound of smearcase until smooth, add three tablespoonfuls of thick cream and two of melted butter; season with pepper and salt. Spread some of this cheese mixture on a buttered slice of pumpernickel bread, followed by a slice of rye covered with the cheese, covered with a slice of buttered white bread. Garnish with slice of pickle.

PARMESAN SANDWICH

Finely grated Parmesan cheese, a dash of salt and pepper, one tablespoonful of tomato catsup, mix and place between squares of unsweetened cracker.

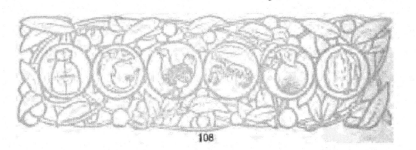

Put crackers on a thin plate, set in hot oven for three minutes or until the cheese melts and the cracker becomes crisp. Serve hot.

PARMESAN AND RADISH SANDWICH

Peel radishes and chop very fine; place on ice until needed; then mix with a very little whipped cream; spread the mixture between thin oblongs of brown bread, dust a little grated Parmesan cheese over the top before the second slice is put on.

PARMESAN AND CELERY SANDWICH

Whip a gill of cream, add to it sufficient grated cheese, American or Parmesan, to make a stiff paste; spread lightly buttered white bread with this and sprinkle thickly with very finely minced celery. Cover with another slice of buttered bread.

SEAFOAM SANDWICH

Spread crisp seafoam crackers with butter, a sprinkling of grated Parmesan cheese, and very finely chopped celery or olives. Place two together and serve.

FRENCH CHEESE SANDWICH

Slice brown bread very thin, butter, lay thinly sliced cheese on top, and spread over cheese a thick layer of any kind of jam, and cover with another slice of bread.

MOROCCO SANDWICH

Melt a cupful of cheese, American or Parmesan; while soft, add enough mayonnaise to make it spread easily; lay this on thin slices of lightly buttered whole wheat bread and slice stuffed olives over cheese. Cover with another slice of lightly buttered bread; garnish top with stuffed olive.

CLUB HOUSE SANDWICH

Rub to a paste one tablespoonful of butter and two tablespoonfuls of soft club house cheese, a tablespoonful of grated Parmesan, a dash of salt and pepper, a teaspoonful of tarragon vinegar, and a teaspoonful of anchovy paste. Spread the above mixture on thin slices of toasted bread. Put slices together and cut triangular.

COTTAGE SANDWICH

Cut slices of brown bread, do not remove crusts; rub half a pint of cottage cheese to a smooth paste, then press it through fine sieve. Add two tablespoonfuls of melted butter, slowly beating the while, add half a teaspoonful of salt, and two tablespoonfuls of thick cream; spread each slice of the bread with mixture; cover with another thin slice of white bread and on top of that another thin layer of cheese; place a slice of brown bread on top and trim into shape. Garnish with an olive.

COTTAGE SANDWICH NO. 2

On thin slices of lightly buttered graham bread spread cottage cheese that has been mixed with a little chopped chives. Cover with another slice of bread.

GRUYERE SANDWICH

Cut rye and white bread in very thin slices and spread sparingly with butter; cut cold tongue and gruyere cheese in thin slices; on white bread arrange the tongue, rye bread over tongue and cheese over rye bread; repeat, put under a weight and let stand for two hours; then cut crosswise in thin slices. Garnish with olive.

COTTAGE AND OLIVE SANDWICH

Spread thin slices of lightly buttered graham bread with mustard, then a thin layer of cottage cheese, and then a layer of chopped olives that have been mixed with a little mayonnaise dressing. Cover with another slice of bread and press together.

BOHEMIAN SANDWICH

On thin slices of lightly buttered graham bread, spread a thin layer of mustard; on top of that spread a layer of cottage cheese, then a layer of olives that have been chopped fine, and mixed with a little mayonnaise dressing. Cover with another slice of bread and press together. Cut in strips and serve on a lettuce leaf.

DUTCH SANDWICH

Between thin slices of lightly buttered rye bread, spread highly seasoned cottage cheese; on this sprinkle finely chopped olives. Cut in diamond shape. Garnish with a sprig of parsley.

WAUKESHA CHEESE SANDWICH

Cream one brick of Waukesha cheese with a little sweet cream, add a pinch of salt, a few chopped pecan nut meats, and a few chopped olives. Place between thin slices of lightly buttered rye bread.

IMPERIAL CHEESE SANDWICH

One-half jar of Imperial cheese, one-half bottle (small size) of stuffed olives sliced fine, four table-spoonfuls of cream. Mix well and spread on thin slices of lightly buttered white bread with a crisp lettuce leaf between the slices.

SWISS CHEESE SANDWICH

Cut rye bread very thin. Spread lightly with butter. Between the pieces place thin slices of Swiss cheese. Spread with mustard. Garnish with a dill pickle sliced thin.

SWISS CHEESE SANDWICH NO. 2

Butter thin slices of pumpernickel bread. Between slices put a thin layer of Swiss cheese and leaves of watercress. Cut in long narrow strips. Garnish with an olive.

GREEN CHEESE SANDWICH

Spread on thin slices of lightly buttered white bread, green cheese grated fine. Put slices together and garnish with a sour pickle.

SWISS AND NUT SANDWICH

Chop English walnuts fine; mix with grated Swiss cheese. Add a little thick cream to moisten, season with salt and cayenne. Place between thin slices of lightly buttered brown bread. Garnish with an olive.

CREAM CHEESE AND OLIVE SAND-WICH

Work cream cheese until smooth, add one-half quantity of chopped olives, season with salt, and moisten with mayonnaise. Place between thin slices of lightly buttered rye bread.

CREAM CHEESE AND OLIVE SANDWICH NO. 2

Chop olives fine, mix with cream cheese, add a little sweet cream to moisten, season with salt and paprika. Place between thin slices of lightly buttered white or brown bread.

DAIRY SANDWICH

On thin slices of Swiss cheese, spread fresh butter and put the two slices together.

CREAM CHEESE AND PIMOLAS SANDWICH

Mix one cream cheese with an equal amount of chopped pimolas; season with salt and cayenne, and moisten with a little mayonnaise dressing. Place between thin slices of lightly buttered white or brown bread.

116

CREAM CHEESE AND PINEAPPLE SANDWICH

Chop the pineapple fine and drain. Spread lightly buttered white bread thinly with cream cheese; sprinkle with pineapple and press together, then cut the sandwiches in thin, slender strips.

CREAM CHEESE AND WALNUT SANDWICH

One cup of walnut meats, chopped fine; add enough cream cheese to make a paste; add salt and a bit of red pepper. Place between lightly buttered white bread cut in fancy shapes.

CREAM CHEESE AND NUT SANDWICH

Chop English walnuts fine, mix with cream cheese and a little chopped celery; add a dash of mayonnaise dressing. Place the mixture between thin slices of lightly buttered white bread. Garnish with a sprig of watercress.

CREAM CHEESE AND BEET SANDWICH

On thin slices of lightly buttered white bread, lay a crisp lettuce leaf; on that spread cream cheese, on top of the cheese sprinkle chopped pickled beets. Cover with another slice of buttered bread.

CREAM CHEESE AND CUCUMBER SANDWICH

On thin slices of lightly buttered brown bread spread cream cheese; over same sprinkle chopped cucumbers that have been mixed with a little French dressing. Cover with another slice of lightly buttered brown bread.

CREAM CHEESE AND GUAVA JELLY SANDWICH

Spread an equal number of slices of lightly buttered white bread with guava jelly and cream cheese. Put slices together and trim the edges.

CREAM CHEESE AND GREEN PEP-PER SANDWICH

Spread lightly buttered white bread with cream cheese; on this lay thin slices of green pepper that have been dipped in mayonnaise dressing. Cover with another slice of bread, cut oblong, and garnish with a sprig of parsley and an olive.

CREAM CHEESE AND PARSLEY SANDWICH

Spread thin slices of Boston brown bread lightly buttered, with cream cheese, mixed with a little chopped parsley. Put two slices together and garnish with an olive.

CREAM CHEESE AND LETTUCE SANDWICH

Slice white bread very thin, when you have pared off the crust. Butter smoothly and lightly. Spread

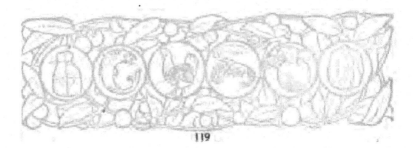

one slice with cream cheese and lay upon the other a crisp lettuce leaf that has been dipped in mayonnaise dressing. Put slices together. Garnish with an olive.

CHEESE AND BAR-LE-DUC CURRANT SANDWICH

Spread thin slices of lightly buttered white bread with cream cheese; sprinkle currants over the cheese; then a teaspoonful of maple syrup. Cover with another slice of bread.

TOASTED WAFERS WITH CREAM CHEESE

Mix a cream cheese with cream and paprika to make a mixture that is soft and yet will hold its shape. Just before serving, toast the wafers and press a star of cheese upon each. (Use a star tube.) Finish with a slice of pimola.

RUSSIAN SANDWICH

Spread zepherettes with cream cheese and cover with chopped olives mixed with a little mayonnaise. Place a zepherette over each and press together.

ORIENTAL SANDWICH

Mix one cake of cream cheese with a little maple syrup, then add sliced maraschino cherries. Place between thin slices of lightly buttered bread. Garnish with a spray of smilax and a cherry.

DAINTY CHEESE SANDWICH

A dainty cheese sandwich to serve at afternoon parties is made by placing the halves of an English walnut on either side of a square of cream cheese. Serve on a crisp lettuce leaf.

MACAROON SANDWICH

Be sure the macaroons are fresh. Lay a slice of fresh cream cheese between two macaroons, pressing them firmly together. Keep in a cool place until wanted.

FAIRMONT SANDWICHES

Work a small cream cheese until smooth, using a wooden spoon, and season with salt. Chop red and green peppers separately and wring in cheese-cloth to remove some of the moisture. Mix one-half of the cheese with some of the red pepper, the other half the green pepper. Spread four thin slices of white bread sparingly with butter, on the lower slice spread the green pepper mixture, cover with another slice of bread, on top of that spread a layer of the red pepper mixture, cover with the third slice and spread that with the green pepper mixture. Cover with the fourth slice of bread. Fold in cheese-cloth and press under a weight, then cut in thin slices downward.

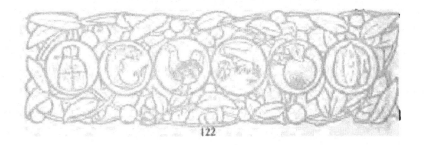

ITALIAN SANDWICH

Take an equal number of slices of white and graham bread, spread with butter and cream cheese; on these put finely chopped olives that have been mixed with a little mayonnaise dressing. Press slices together in pairs with a crisp lettuce leaf between each pair, and cut diagonally. Garnish with parsley.

BUFFET SANDWICH

One teacupful grated American or Parmesan cheese, one tablespoonful of melted butter, one teaspoonful of made mustard, a little salt and pepper. Mix well, spread on thin slices of lightly buttered rye bread. Put two slices together and cut in triangles.

BUMMERS CUSTARD SANDWICH

Take a cake of Roquefort cheese and divide in thirds; moisten one third with brandy, another third with olive oil, and the other third with Worcestershire sauce. Mix all together and place between split water biscuits toasted. Good for a stag lunch.

NUT

ENGLISH WALNUT SANDWICH

Chop English walnuts fine, and over them pour the following dressing; five yolks of eggs well beaten, juice of two lemons, a good half-cup of water, one teaspoonful of sugar, and a pinch of salt. Let it cook until the eggs thicken. When cool, place between thin slices of lightly buttered white bread.

ENGLISH WALNUT SANDWICH NO. 2

Chop fine a cupful of English walnut meats; moisten with a little thick cream and place between a slice of brown bread and one of white lightly buttered. Cut in rounds with a biscuit cutter.

ENGLISH WALNUT SANDWICH NO. 3

Chop English walnuts fine; moisten with a little mayonnaise dressing, and place between thin slices of lightly buttered brown bread.

ENGLISH WALNUT AND FIG SANDWICH

Chop figs fine, adding enough water to make a smooth paste, and cook slowly until of a consistency to spread. Flavor with a little orange juice or grated candied orange peel. Chop one-half cup of English walnuts fine, add to the fig paste filling. Place between thin slices of white or brown bread lightly buttered, cut in fanciful shapes.

ENGLISH WALNUT AND GINGER SANDWICH

Three thin slices of lightly buttered white bread; between the first and second place a layer of chopped, preserved ginger, mixed with a little thick cream; and between the second and third slices, place a layer of chopped English walnuts; then tie up each sandwich neatly with blue baby ribbon.

ENGLISH WALNUT AND RAISIN SANDWICH

Chop equal quantities of English walnuts and raisins fine, mix with a little cream, and place between thin slices of lightly buttered white bread. Garnish top with a raisin.

ENGLISH WALNUT AND DATE SANDWICH

Chop English walnut meats fine, mix with an equal amount of chopped dates; moisten with a little whipped cream and place mixture between buttered crackers or thin slices of white bread.

SALTED ENGLISH WALNUT SANDWICH

Spread thin slices of Boston brown bread with butter; then chop English walnuts fine, sprinkle with salt, and put a layer of the nuts between two slices of bread.

BLACK WALNUT SANDWICH

Between thin slices of lightly buttered brown bread spread black walnut meats chopped rather fine. Nice to serve with hot chocolate.

CHESTNUT SANDWICH

Shell and blanch the chestnuts, then boil fifteen minutes; drain and cool, and when cool chop fine. Add an equal quantity of finely chopped celery, moisten with a little French dressing, mix, and put between thin slices of lightly buttered white bread, with a crisp lettuce leaf between.

PECAN SANDWICH

One cup of chopped pecans, one cup of chopped dates, mixed with a tablespoonful of whipped cream to moisten. Place between thin slices of white or whole wheat bread.

PECAN SANDWICH NO. 2

Chop pecan nuts very fine, moisten with a little mayonnaise dressing and place between thin slices of lightly buttered white bread.

PECAN SANDWICH NO. 3

Mix one cup of finely chopped pecan nuts with a little chutney. Place between thin slices of buttered white bread.

PECAN AND ENGLISH WALNUT SANDWICH

Chop fine one-half cup each of pecan and walnut meats, add one-half cup of olives stoned and chopped fine, moisten with a little mayonnaise dressing and place between thin slices of lightly buttered graham bread.

HICKORY NUT SANDWICH

Mix together chopped hickory nuts and pot cheese, add a dash of paprika, and place between thin slices of either white or brown bread lightly buttered. Garnish with an olive.

HICKORY NUT AND CHEESE SANDWICH

Beat to a cream one tablespoonful of butter, then add three heaping tablespoonfuls of cream cheese. Mix thoroughly, adding a little sweet cream if necessary to make creamy. Chop a quarter-pound of hickory nuts fine, and blend with the cheese paste; season with salt, pepper, and a little lemon juice. Spread on thin slices of brown bread. Put two slices together and garnish with an olive.

PEANUT SANDWICH

Chop roasted and salted peanuts, mix with a little mayonnaise dressing, place between thin slices of lightly buttered entire wheat bread.

PEANUT SANDWICH NO. 2

Chop a cup of freshly roasted shelled peanuts very fine, mix with three tablespoonfuls of mayonnaise dressing, add salt to taste, and sprinkle upon lightly buttered slices of white bread. Put slices together and cut in tiny squares.

PEANUT SANDWICH NO. 3

Chop peanuts fine or put through a coffee mill, salt to taste, and add a little sherry or port wine to make a thick paste. Spread on thin slices of lightly buttered white bread. Put two slices together and garnish with a candied cherry.

PEANUT SANDWICH NO. 4

Cut white bread in rounds with the biscuit cutter, cover with whipped cream slightly sweetened. Sprinkle chopped peanuts over the cream. Cover with another round of bread and serve as soon as made.

PEANUT AND BANANA SAND-WICH

Between thin slices of lightly buttered white bread place a crisp lettuce leaf that has been dipped in mayonnaise dressing; on this place slices. of banana and sprinkle with ground peanuts.

PEANUT MAYONNAISE SAND-WICH

Heat a tablespoonful of butter in a pan and add the juice of a lemon. Season with salt and pepper. To this gradually add a well beaten egg, thinned with sour cream, adding it slowly, stirring the while to prevent it from curdling. When it begins to thicken, remove and stir in enough ground peanuts to make a good spreading butter. In preparing sandwiches of this, cut bread thin, spread with the mayonnaise; and lay between the slices a crisp lettuce leaf. Cut the sandwiches in fancy shapes. Dainty for noon-day luncheon.

ALMOND SANDWICH

Cut white bread in rounds and lightly butter, put on a layer of finely chopped almonds, add a sprinkling of salt and a dash of lemon juice; cover with another round of bread and press a blanched nut in the centre. Serve on a lettuce leaf.

ALMOND SANDWICH NO. 2

Whip one-half gill of sweet cream to a stiff froth; add one-half pound of almonds, blanched and pounded to a paste, with a little rose or orange flower water; add two tablespoonfuls of sugar and spread over thin slices of white bread; roll into tiny cylinders or cut in narrow strips.

ALMOND SANDWICH NO. 3

On thin slices of buttered Boston brown bread sprinkle finely chopped almonds, cover with another slice of bread, and cut in squares.

ALMOND AND CELERY SANDWICH

Chop almonds fine and mix with twice the bulk of finely chopped celery; moisten with a little mayonnaise dressing and put between thin slices of lightly buttered white bread.

ALMOND AND LEMON SANDWICH

Grate the thin yellow rind of one lemon, being careful not to rub off any of the bitter white pith; blanch and pound one-half pound of almonds, adding slowly the juice of one lemon. When a smooth paste is formed, add the grated lemon rind. Rub the yolks of two hard-boiled eggs to a smooth paste, add the almond mixture, and spread over thin slices of lightly buttered white bread. Cover with another slice of bread and cut in triangles.

TOASTED ALMOND SANDWICH

Toast almonds to a light brown and grate; form into a paste with a little lemon juice, add a little salt, spread on thin slices of lightly buttered white bread and cover with another slice and cut in strips.

SWEET

ORANGE SANDWICH

Between thin slices of lightly buttered white bread place thin slices of orange that have been lightly dusted with powdered sugar.

ORANGE MARMALADE SAND-WICH

Spread thinly buttered white bread with orange marmalade. Put two slices together and cut the sandwich in slender strips.

ORANGE MARMALADE SAND-WICH NO. 2

On thin slices of lightly buttered white bread spread orange marmalade. Put four slices together, put under a weight and when well pressed, trim off the crusts and cut down in thin slices. Serve on lace paper doily.

DAINTY RIBBON SANDWICH

Cut the crust from a loaf of white and of brown bread. Cut three slices one-half inch thick from each loaf. Spread with butter and orange marmalade. Put six slices together and press firmly. Trim the edges evenly, then with a sharp knife cut into slices about three-quarters of an inch thick. Place the sandwich on a lace paper doily. Serve as soon as made.

GEM SANDWICH

Grate orange peel very fine, add a dash of ginger, spread thin slices of buttered white bread with Neufchatel cheese, sprinkle orange peel and ginger over the cheese. Put slices together. Garnish with an olive.

LEMON SANDWICH

Slice a lemon very thin and remove the rind, sprinkle with powdered sugar and place between thin slices of lightly buttered white bread cut round. Garnish top with a candied cherry.

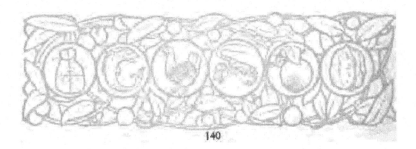

FRUIT SANDWICH

Spread thin slices of white bread with chocolate cream butter, on this place a layer of fresh fruit such as bananas, strawberries, or raspberries; cover with another slice, and garnish top with a sugared berry.

STRAWBERRY SANDWICH

Between thin slices of lightly buttered white bread, place strawberries cut in halves, sprinkle with powdered sugar. Garnish top of sandwich with a whole sugared berry.

GRAPE SANDWICH

Remove skins and seeds from one pound of white grapes. Chop grapes, one large apple, and two stalks of celery fine. Mix with a little French dressing and place between thin slices of lightly buttered white bread. Cut sandwiches in strips.

RED RASPBERRY SANDWICH

Mix berries with thick cream and a little powdered sugar and place between thinly cut slices of buttered white bread. Garnish top with a berry.

APPLE SANDWICH

Between thin slices of buttered white bread place thin slices of tart apples, which have been steeped for an hour in a mixture of lemon juice and sugar.

APPLE SANDWICH NO. 2

On thin slices of lightly buttered white bread spread baked apple. Dust with powdered sugar. Cover with another slice of bread and cut in strips.

APPLE BUTTER SANDWICH

On thin slices of lightly buttered white bread, spread apple butter. Sprinkle chopped candied orange peel, cover with another slice of bread.

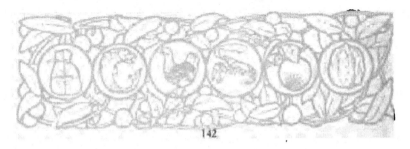

PINEAPPLE SANDWICH

One cup of pineapple cut fine, two tablespoonfuls of lemon juice, and one cupful of sugar. Cook until thick, and when cold spread upon lady fingers and press together. White bread may be used.

CHERRY SANDWICH

One cup of maraschino cherries cut in small pieces, mixed with one-half cup of English walnuts chopped fine. Moisten with whipped cream. Spread on thin slices of white buttered bread, put two slices together and cut in squares. Garnish with a maraschino cherry.

CHERRY SANDWICH NO. 2

Chop a quarter of a pound of candied cherries fine; add a few drops of sherry. Mix and spread on rounds of lightly buttered white bread. Cover with another slice and garnish with a candied cherry.

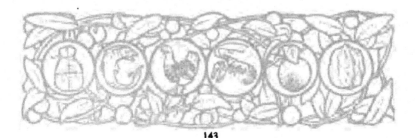

CANDIED CHERRY SANDWICH

Chop candied cherries very fine, add as many seeded raisins chopped fine, moisten with orange juice. Mix to a paste and spread on thin slices of white bread lightly buttered. Put two slices together and garnish top with a cherry.

CANDIED CHERRY SANDWICH NO. 2

Chop candied cherries fine, moisten with orange juice, place between thin slices of lightly buttered white bread. Garnish top with a cherry.

CREAM AND CANDIED FRUIT SANDWICH

Cut candied cherries fine and moisten with a few drops of wine. Cut sponge cake in squares and cover with whipped cream that has been sweetened and

flavored and chilled; on top of this sprinkle the candied cherries. Cover with another piece of the cake and serve at once.

CAKE AND CANDIED CHERRY SANDWICH

Cut sponge cake into slices a quarter of an inch thick; cut the slices into rounds. Chop candied cherries fine, moisten with a little orange juice. Spread the mixture on the rounds of cake; press two pieces together. Garnish with a candied cherry.

TUTTI-FRUTTI SANDWICH

Chop candied cherries, peaches, and apricots, add a little sherry wine and mix to a paste. Spread on thin slices of lightly buttered white bread, cover with another slice and cut in strips.

BANANA SANDWICH

Mash ripe bananas; add a dash of lemon juice; sweeten to taste. Place between thin slices of buttered white bread cut oblong.

BANANA SANDWICH NO. 2

On thin slices of lightly buttered white bread spread mayonnaise dressing then add thin slices of bananas; cover with another slice of bread. Serve on a lettuce leaf.

BANANA AND CHERRY SAND-WICH

Mash three bananas fine, add one-half cup of chopped maraschino cherries, a tablespoonful of powdered sugar, moisten with a little thick cream, mix, and place between thin slices of lightly buttered white bread. Garnish with a cherry.

BANANA TOAST SANDWICH

Between thin slices of lightly buttered graham bread, place three slices of banana; toast quickly to a light brown. Serve hot.

BANANA AND TOASTED BROWN BREAD SANDWICH

Between thin slices of buttered brown bread from which the crusts have been removed, place slices of banana, press together and place in the oven and leave until bread is toasted. Serve hot. Very good for invalids.

ORIENTAL SANDWICH

Mash four bananas; add one-half cup of maraschino cherries, two tablespoonfuls of honey, and two tablespoonfuls of sweet thick cream. Mix and spread on thin slices of lightly buttered white bread, cover with another slice, and garnish top with a cherry.

FIVE O'CLOCK TEA

Mash bananas fine, add an equal amount of mashed red raspberries, moisten with a little sweet thick cream. Place between thin slices of lightly buttered white bread. Cut in fancy shapes.

FIG SANDWICH

Chop figs fine, moisten with a little maple syrup and work to a paste; spread mixture on thin slices of lightly buttered white bread, roll, and tie with baby ribbon.

FIG SANDWICH NO. 2

One-half pound of finely chopped figs, one-third cup of sugar, half-cup of boiling water, and two tablespoonfuls of lemon juice; mix these ingredients and cook in a double boiler until thick. When cool spread mixture on thin slices of buttered white bread, cover with another slice and cut in fancy shapes.

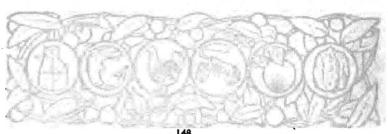

FIG SANDWICH NO. 3

Stew figs and chop; season with a little wine and place between lightly buttered slices of white or graham bread.

FAVORITE SANDWICH

Chop stewed figs, add a dash of lemon juice, spread on thin slices of lightly buttered white bread, and cover with another slice. Garnish with a spray of smilax.

FIG AND NUT SANDWICH

Cut rounds of bread with a biscuit cutter and lightly butter. For each sandwich use two dried figs, fill the figs with the English walnut meats chopped; roll the figs in powdered sugar and place between the rounds of bread.

FIG AND NUT SANDWICH NO. 2

Chop figs and English walnuts fine; moisten with whipped cream; place between thin slices of lightly buttered white bread. Garnish with smilax.

FIG AND ROLL

Split twelve figs, scrape out the soft portion and rub this to a paste; butter thin slices of fresh white or brown bread, remove the crust, spread on the fig paste and roll the bread carefully; press for a moment, then roll it in a piece of tissue paper, pressing the ends as you would an old-fashioned motto, or it may be tied with baby ribbon of any color.

LADY FINGER SANDWICH

Chop figs fine and rub to a smooth paste; add a dash of orange juice and spread on lady fingers; press two fingers together and garnish with a spray of smilax.

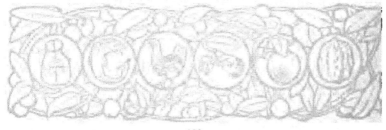

DATE AND FIG SANDWICH

To two cups of dates with stones removed, add one cup of washed figs, also one cup of seeded raisins; chop very fine and add enough water to make a paste to spread easily. Let this boil one minute, and when cool spread between thin slices of buttered white bread, cover with another slice and garnish top with a sugared date.

DATE AND NUT SANDWICH

Between slices of brown bread lightly buttered and cut thin, place this filling; dates stoned and chopped fine, walnut meats chopped fine, moistened with a little sherry wine. Garnish with a spray of smilax.

DATE AND ORANGE SANDWICH

Remove the pulp and inner skin from six oranges, cut into small pieces, add one pound of chopped dates and a half-cup of walnut meats chopped fine; add half-

cup of powdered sugar, moisten with a little sherry or port wine, and place the mixture between slices of lightly buttered white bread.

RAISIN SANDWICH

Cut large raisins in halves with a sharp knife; take out the seeds, dip in brandy or sherry; do not let them remain a moment in the liquor; cut white bread in rounds, spread with butter, and put a layer of raisins between the two rounds of bread. Garnish top with a raisin and serve with lemonade.

FRUIT JELLY SANDWICH

Soak one box of gelatine in one cup of cold water, and dissolve it in one cup of boiling water. Add one cup of sugar, one-half cup of lemon juice, one cup of orange juice, and half a cup of mashed red raspberries. When cool spread on squares of sponge cake, or thinly cut and lightly buttered white bread. Cover with another slice.

JELLY AND NUT SANDWICH

Chop English walnuts fine and stir into whipped cream; spread currant jelly on thin slices of lightly buttered white bread; on top of that spread the walnuts and cream, cover that with currant jelly, and lastly cover with another slice of bread. Serve as soon as made.

CURRANT JELLY SANDWICH

Cut fresh bread in as thin slices as possible. Butter them evenly, spread with currant jelly and sprinkle with fresh grated cocoanut; roll each slice separately and tie the roll with baby ribbon. Make when ready to serve.

CURRANT JELLY AND ENGLISH WALNUT SANDWICH

Spread thin slices of lightly buttered white bread with currant jelly and sprinkle with finely chopped English walnut meats. Cover with another slice and cut in oblong shape.

TOMATO JELLY SANDWICH

One cupful of boiled and strained tomatoes, seasoned with salt, pepper, paprika and a little tabasco sauce. Dissolve quarter box of gelatine in one-half cup of water, add to the tomatoes, and mix thoroughly. Cool in forms that will slice in shape of sandwiches to be used. Place between thin slices of lightly buttered white bread.

QUINCE JELLY AND NUT SAND-WICH

Mix a cupful of quince jelly with half a cupful of finely chopped hickory or pecan nuts and spread on thin slices of lightly buttered white bread. Cover with another slice and cut in squares.

QUINCE JELLY SANDWICH

Spread thin slices of lightly buttered white bread with quince jelly. Put slices together, cut in squares, and garnish with a spray of maidenhair fern.

GOOSEBERRY JAM SANDWICH

Spread thinly cut slices of lightly buttered white bread with gooseberry jam; place slices together and cut in slender strips. Garnish with a spray of smilax. Serve as soon as made.

CLARET JELLY SANDWICH

Soak one box of gelatine in one cup of cold water, then dissolve in one cup of boiling water, add one cup of sugar and strain. When cold, add the juice of half a lemon, and one cup of claret and set in a cool place. When ready for use, cover thin slices of lightly buttered white bread with the jelly, cover with another slice of buttered bread and cut in strips.

MARBLED BREAD SANDWICH

Make an equal number of white and brown bread sandwiches, lightly spread with butter and currant jelly, press sandwiches together in alternating colors, cut in thin strips. Serve on lace paper doily.

BANANA SANDWICH

Place peeled bananas, sliced across, between thin slices of buttered brown bread from which the crusts have been trimmed. Place in the oven and leave until bread is toasted and you will have delicious and nourishing hot sandwiches. Very good for invalids.

MARRON SANDWICH

Cut the bread in rounds with a biscuit cutter; put a *marron glace* in the centre and around it whipped cream that has been sweetened and flavored. Nice for afternoon luncheon.

HONEY SANDWICH

Spread thinly cut slices of lightly buttered white bread with honey; put slices together and garnish with a pansy. Serve as soon as made.

HONEY AND BANANA SANDWICH

Mixed strained honey with mashed ripe bananas; place between thinly cut slices of buttered white bread.

FRENCH TEA SANDWICH

On thinly cut slices of lightly buttered white bread cut round, spread cream cheese and currant jelly. Cover with another slice and sprinkle top of sandwich with crumbs of pistache.

DAINTY PEANUT SANDWICH

One cup of sugar and enough water to cover; boil until it threads from spoon; stir this into the white of an egg beaten stiff. Add one cup of peanuts ground fine; spread the paste on salted wafers; let stand a while before serving.

VERANDA SANDWICH

Chop crystallized ginger fine, moisten with a dash of orange juice; place between thin slices of lightly buttered white bread; cut in fancy shapes and garnish each with a spray of smilax.

PUFF PASTE SANDWICH

Roll puff paste very thin; cut round with a biscuit cutter; bake to a delicate brown. Add chopped almonds to apple or peach marmalade and place the mixture between two rounds of pastry.

DREAM SANDWICH

Cold chopped boiled sweetened prunes, mix with English walnuts chopped fine, moisten with a little of the prune syrup, and place between thin slices of lightly buttered white bread. Garnish with a spray of smilax.

CHOCOLATE SANDWICH

Melt a teaspoonful of butter in a saucepan, stir into it all the unsweetened chocolate (bitter) it will take up. Grate the chocolate directly into the butter. Stir until butter and chocolate are thoroughly mixed. Take from the fire and let it get cold before spreading on thin slices of graham bread, lightly buttered. Cover with another slice and cut in strips.

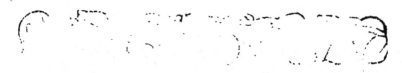

CHOCOLATE AND NUT SANDWICH

Take two tablespoonfuls of sweetened chocolate, mix with a little water and heat to a thick paste; chop fine a half-pint of English walnuts or hickory nuts, stir the chocolate paste when cooling, add the nuts, and spread thinly on narrow wafers. Let harden, then press the two wafers together.

MAPLE CREAM SANDWICH

One-half pound of maple sugar, one-half pound of brown sugar, one-half cup of water, and one-half teaspoonful of cream of tartar; boil these together until they form a soft ball when dipped into cold water. When nearly cold, beat with a fork until thick and creamy; spread on an equal number of thin round slices of buttered white and entire wheat bread, and place together in pairs, one of each kind of bread.

MAPLE SUGAR SANDWICH

On thin slices of lightly buttered white bread spread maple sugar, put slices together and cut with a maple leaf cutter. Serve with hot coffee.

LOG CABIN SANDWICH

Boil one cupful of maple syrup, one-half cupful chopped dates, one-half cupful chopped almonds, one-half cupful pineapple together, let cook for five minutes, take from fire, and add teaspoonful of lemon juice. Cut the bread in long thin strips and remove the crust. Spread with the mixture. Put slices together and wrap in oiled paper; let stand a few hours, when the paper can be removed and they will keep the shape desired.

GINGER SANDWICH

On thin slices of lightly buttered graham bread, sprinkle finely chopped Canton ginger; press slices together.

GINGER AND ORANGE SANDWICH

Soften Neufchatel cheese with a little cream; spread on thin slices of white bread and cover with

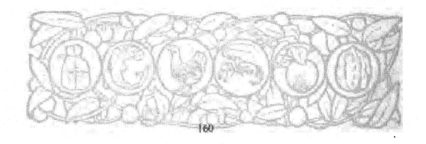

finely minced candied orange peel and preserved ginger; cover with another slice of bread and garnish with a spray of maidenhair fern.

CHESTNUT AND PRUNE SANDWICH

Boil chestnuts twenty minutes; peel and chop fine, add an equal amount of cooked prunes chopped; moisten with a little cream and place between thin slices of lightly buttered whole wheat bread. Garnish top with a maraschino cherry.

HALLOWE'EN SANDWICH

One cup of celery, one orange cut fine, one-half cup of raisins seeded and halved; add one-half cup of grated apple to one-half cup of mayonnaise and mix with this; place between thin slices of lightly buttered white or whole wheat bread. Garnish with a spray of smilax.

INDIA SANDWICH

One cup each preserved ginger and candied orange peel chopped fine; mix with one-half cup of thick cream and spread on white bread thinly buttered. Garnish with stick of candied orange peel.

WHIPPED CREAM SANDWICH

One cup of thick cream, one tablespoonful of powdered sugar. Beat until solid, then add three drops of vanilla, let it become chilled, then spread on lady fingers, press together and serve as soon as made.

SCHOOL SANDWICH

On thin slices of lightly buttered white bread, spread brown sugar; cover with another slice of bread and wrap in wax paper.

COCOANUT SANDWICH

One and one-half cup of grated cocoanut, one-half cup of English walnuts chopped fine, one tablespoonful of rose water, three tablespoonfuls of sugar; mix well, moisten with three tablespoonfuls of thick cream. Spread mixture on thin slices of buttered white bread, cover with another slice and cut in strips.

COCOANUT SANDWICH NO. 2

Roll out one-half pound of puff paste until one-fourth of an inch thick, then place it in a baking tin and bake in a hot oven until a golden brown; when done, let it get cold; whip one-half pint of cream to a stiff dry froth, add to it three tablespoonfuls each of powdered white sugar and desiccated cocoanut. Cut the pastry into strips three inches long by one inch wide; spread some of the cocoanut cream on each piece, put two pieces together and sprinkle powdered white sugar thickly over them.

NUT AND FRUIT SANDWICH

Mash half-pound of pitted prunes, mix them with a half-pound of seedless raisins, half-pound of stoned dates, and the same quantity of washed figs, quarter of a pound of blanched almonds, a quarter of a pound of peeled Brazil nuts, and one pound of pecans. Put through the meat chopper, add the juice of two oranges and knead the mixture with your hands; pack it down into baking powder boxes or into any round tin and stand it aside in a cold place; when wanted for use, remove from the tins, cut thin, and place slices between lightly buttered white bread cut round. Garnish top with a maraschino cherry.

FUDGE SANDWICH

Melt on tin in oven, fudge or fresh chocolate creams until soft enough to be spread; spread wafer crackers with this filling, tie each two with white baby ribbon. Serve with lemonade.

VIOLET SANDWICH

Cover the butter with violets over night; slice white bread thin and spread with the butter; put slices together and cover with the petals of the violets.

ROSE-LEAF SANDWICH

Flavor fresh unsalted butter with rose by packing in closed jar with a layer of rose leaves and leaving several hours. Any fragrant rose will answer. Cut white bread into dainty strips or circles, spread with the perfumed butter, put one or two rose leaves between the slices, allowing the edges to show.

CLOVER SANDWICH

Trim the crust from a loaf of bread and place bread in a stone jar with clover blossoms; wrap the butter in cheese-cloth and also place in the jar; leave over night. Cut the bread thin and spread with the clover-scented butter; put two slices together and garnish with a clover blossom.

NASTURTIUM SANDWICH

Cover the bread and butter with nasturtium flowers over night; cut white bread thin and spread lightly with the butter. Put two nasturtium flowers between the slices.

CHINESE NUT SANDWICH

Stone two cups of Chinese nuts, moisten with three tablespoonfuls of thick cream, sweetened with a little honey; spread on slices of lightly buttered white bread. Cover with another slice and cut in squares.

CREAM SANDWICH

Cream four ounces of butter, add gradually four ounces of brown sugar, four ounces of fine flour, four eggs one by one, a squeeze of lemon juice or a tablespoonful of rose water, and lastly a teaspoonful of baking powder. When thoroughly mixed, bake in shallow tins. Whip up till perfectly thick a quarter of a pint of cream, spread this on half the strips and cover with the other sandwich-fashion. Ice these sandwiches over with chocolate icing.

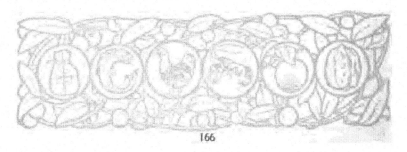

MISCELLANEOUS

BOSTON BAKED BEAN SANDWICH

Press cold baked beans through a colander, add two stalks of celery chopped fine, a teaspoonful of horse-radish, and a little tomato catsup; mix and spread on buttered slices of Boston brown bread, cover with another slice, and garnish with a radish and a pickle.

NEW ENGLAND SANDWICH

Mash beans that have been cooked well, add a dash of catsup, lay on a crisp lettuce leaf between lightly buttered white or brown bread. Garnish with a pickle.

MEXICAN SANDWICH

Put large square salted crackers into the oven to heat. When warm, put on each cracker a large table-spoonful of baked beans that has been mixed with a little catsup heated with butter and highly seasoned.

POTATO SANDWICH

Run three good sized boiled potatoes through the potato ricer, season with salt and pepper, add the yolks of four hard-boiled eggs that have been rubbed to a paste, and one tablespoonful of melted butter. Mix thoroughly and place between thin slices of lightly buttered brown bread. Garnish with a pickle.

POTATO AND HAM SANDWICH

Into a pint of well seasoned mashed potatoes, stir two eggs without beating; spread two tablespoonfuls of this potato out smoothly, and lay on it a slice of neatly trimmed boiled ham. Cover this with the potato, pinch the edges together. Fry in butter until a delicate brown.

RICE SANDWICH

Creole rice may be shaped to a circle, in which make a cavity; leave this to stand in a cool place until firm; when so, cut in half, horizontally. Spread peach

preserves neatly on lower ring, mask well with syrup.
Put on the upper ring and mask well with the syrup.
Put in a cool place until ready to serve; cut V-shape
and serve with unflavored cream.

POPCORN SANDWICH

Pass two cupfuls of freshly popped corn through
the meat chopper, place this in the chopping bowl, add
a dash of salt and cayenne pepper, five boned sardines,
a dash of Worcestershire, and enough tomato catsup
to form a paste. Spread this on circles of hot buttered
toast. Sprinkle with Parmesan cheese and crisp in hot
oven. Serve as soon as made.

DYSPEPTIC SANDWICH

Spread thin slices of gluten bread with peanut butter, mixed with crisp brown bread crumbs, put the two
slices together, and cut in strips.

MOSAIC SANDWICH

Cut two slices each of white and dark graham bread; cream one-quarter cup of butter until white. Spread a slice of white bread with the creamed butter, then place a slice of graham bread on it; then spread graham bread with creamed butter; repeat. Place a light weight on all four slices. When butter hardens remove the weight, then cut in thin slices downward.

SANDWICH ROLLS

Take four cupfuls of light bread dough, spread it on the breadboard and roll thin. Spread this sheet with one cupful of butter, fold it up and roll out again; fold as before and let it stand a few minutes in a warm place. Now roll and fold twice more. Let stand a short time, roll out and cut into biscuits, place in pans, not touching, brush over the tops with a little lard and hot water. Let rise one hour and bake. These are very light and will pull apart in flakes. Any filling may be used.

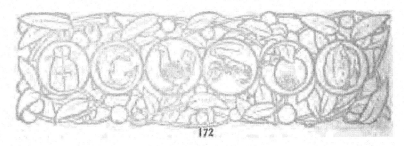

CANAPES

CANAPES

Canapes are *savories*, or appetizers, usually served before the first course at dinners, luncheons, or chafing dish suppers. One slice only is used for each canape. They may be dipped in melted butter, toasted or fried and cut into fancy shapes. The mixture is spread on top, the top is garnished.

CAVIARE CANAPES

Season the caviare with a dash of lemon juice and a very little onion juice. Spread mixture on toasted rounds of white bread and sprinkle top with finely chopped hard-boiled egg. Garnish with cress.

HERRING CANAPES

Toast slices of white bread, remove the crusts and cut oblong. Spread them with butter mixed with a very little French mustard, cover with finely minced sour pickle; place upon each two boneless herrings. Sprinkle finely chopped hard-cooked egg yolk over top.

ANCHOVY CANAPES

Toast rounds of white bread to a nice even brown; place two boneless anchovies on a round of toast, and sprinkle over same the yolks of hard-boiled eggs; dust with white pepper and garnish with a slice of lemon.

LOBSTER CANAPES

Chop the meat of a boiled lobster fine, season with pepper and salt, a dash of lemon juice, and a little mayonnaise dressing and spread on rounds of toasted bread. Garnish with a sprig of parsley.

CRAB CANAPES

Put the contents of a can of crab meat into a saucepan, add one tablespoonful of sherry and let simmer until the liquid disappears. Fry one small finely minced onion in a tablespoonful of butter until brown, add a cupful of milk that has blended with a tablespoonful of flour, let it come to a boil, then add the crab meat and let simmer for ten minutes; remove from the fire and when cool spread on rounds of toast and

sprinkle with grated Parmesan cheese; place in a hot oven until a golden brown. Serve hot.

SARDINE CANAPES

Pound boneless and skinless sardines to a paste; moisten with a little olive oil, and a dash of lemon juice; spread mixture on thin rounds of toasted bread. Arrange leaves of watercress around the edge and put finely chopped hard-boiled egg in the centre.

SARDINE CANAPES NO. 2

Take a box of sardines, remove bone and skin, rub to a paste with three ounces of fresh butter, and gradually add four tablespoonfuls of thick cream, until a paste is formed. Spread the paste over toasted rounds of white bread; sprinkle chopped olives over the whole.

SARDELLEN CANAPES

Toast a thin biscuit cracker and lightly butter. Put a slice of hard-boiled egg in the centre and coil one well cleaned sardellen around the egg. Garnish with a slice of lemon.

SALMON CANAPES

Toast rounds of white bread and spread with melted butter; next with finely flaked salmon, to which add a dash of Worcestershire sauce, and a drop of olive oil; sprinkle finely chopped hard-boiled egg over top. Garnish with a small sprig of parsley.

FISH CANAPES

Rub a quarter of a pound of any kind of cooked fish to a paste; season with pepper and salt, and a few drops of onion juice. Moisten with one tablespoonful of sauce tartare. Spread the above mixture on rounds of buttered brown bread, sprinkle over top finely chopped dill pickles.

HAM CANAPES

Mince and mash to a smooth paste half a pound of cold boiled ham, add two tablespoonfuls of currant jelly, one tablespoon of soft butter, and a half a teaspoon of curry powder or half this amount of paprika if the latter be preferred. Spread this paste on round pieces of toast and garnish with chopped, cooked eggs,

whites and yolks separate, minced pickles, green peppers, and olives.

HAM CANAPES NO. 2

Cut bread in rounds one-fourth inch thick. Saute in butter; spread with finely chopped ham mixed to a paste with a little melted butter and seasoned. Sprinkle top with finely chopped hard-boiled eggs.

BACON CANAPES

Cut bread in squares one-fourth inch thick, saute the bacon fat. Spread with a little French mustard, cover with fried bacon finely chopped, and sprinkle with finely chopped pimolas.

TONGUE CANAPES

Toast one-fourth inch slices of graham bread, cut in rounds and fried in butter; mix cooked tongue that has been chopped fine with creamed butter till it is a paste, and add one tablespoonful of capers to a cupful of tongue. Spread on bread, add a dash of salt and cayenne, and sprinkle with a little finely chopped watercress.

CHICKEN CANAPES

Chop fine the white meat of a chicken and two stalks of celery. Season with salt, pepper, and vinegar. Let stand a few minutes, then drain dry; add a little mayonnaise dressing and mix well. Serve on rounds of toast that have been spread lightly with melted butter. Sprinkle chopped chives over the whole.

NUT AND OLIVE CANAPES

Fry rounds of white bread in butter; mix equal quantities of chopped English walnuts and olives with enough mayonnaise dressing to moisten. Spread on bread and garnish with chopped pimentos.

TOMATO AND CUCUMBER CANAPES

Saute rounds of white bread in butter. Fry slices of tomato in deep fat; place one slice of tomato on each round of bread. Dust with salt and pepper, and lightly spread with mayonnaise dressing followed by a thin slice of cucumber. Sprinkle top with finely chopped hard-boiled egg.

INDEX

LIST OF RECIPES

FISH

EGG

SALAD

MEAT

CHEESE

SWEET

MISCELLANEOUS

CANAPES

CPSIA information can be obtained
at www.ICGtesting.com
Printed in the USA
LVOW06*0749090916

503895LV00007B/55/P